I0631282

Clarence A. Walworth

The Oxford Movement in America

Clarence A. Walworth

The Oxford Movement in America

ISBN/EAN: 9783744653237

Printed in Europe, USA, Canada, Australia, Japan

Cover: Foto ©ninafisch / pixelio.de

More available books at **www.hansebooks.com**

THE

OXFORD MOVEMENT IN AMERICA;

OR,

GLIMPSES OF LIFE

IN AN

ANGLICAN SEMINARY.

BY

REV. CLARENCE E. WALWORTH,

St. Mary's Church, Albany.

New York:
THE CATHOLIC BOOK EXCHANGE,
120 West 60th Street.

CONTENTS.

iii

CHAPTER VIII.

CHAPTER IX.

CHAPTER X.

CHAPTER XI.

CHAPTER XII.

Glimpses of Life in an Anglican Seminary.

CHAPTER I.

FROM LAW TO DIVINITY.—PRESBYTERIANS IN A QUANDARY.—
MY LOCATION AND SURROUNDINGS AT THE SEMINARY.—
EVANGELICAL FRIENDS IN THE CITY.

IN the summer of 1842 I was a practising lawyer in Rochester, N. Y., being the junior member of the firm of Chapin & Walworth. Our office was in a second story front room of the Smith Block, so-called, in Main Street, and directly facing the principal hotel in that city. We were doing a good business and I liked my profession well enough. About that time, however, my mind had been turned towards religion more steadfastly than ever before. I felt growing up within me a strong desire to devote myself entirely to the church. I opened my mind on this subject to the Rev. Dr. Whitehouse, then rector of St. Luke's, and afterwards Bishop of Illinois. I was a member of St. Luke's choir, and a teacher in the Sunday-school, and was strongly attached to the rector. He encouraged me to follow my inclination, as being both rational and deeply settled, and wrote a letter for me to Bishop De Lancey recommending me as a candidate for orders in his diocese.

Neither my father nor any of my friends made any serious opposition to my purpose, and it was carried into speedy execution. My father's personal library of law-books, a large and fine collection, was sent home to him forthwith ; and when I parted with these very little of law remained with me. I myself returned to the family residence at Saratoga Springs, to wait for the opening of the next term of the General Theological Seminary in New York City. I recall only one event which occurred during this interval of any importance to these reminis-

cences. Although it forms no part of my career at the seminary, I introduce it here because it had some influence upon
the development of my mind while there. It brought before
me in a very practical shape the question of clerical and missionary celibacy, a question which afterwards I found much
mooted among my fellow students.

At my father's request I went with him to attend an annual
meeting of the American Board of Foreign Missions. I was
very glad to do this, for the work of spreading the Gospel in
heathen lands had always seemed to me the best and clearest
note of true Christian life in that vague and strangely assorted
thing which Protestants name the church. Our house was always
opened to every one who bore the name of missionary. It was
one of my mother's chief delights to read the pages of the
Missionary Herald, although little was ever found recorded there
except the establishment of some new printing-press, some new
translation and publication of Bibles and tracts into foreign lan-
guages, and new "signs of interest" in some individuals among
the savages who seldom ripened into Christians.

My father also was fond of attending missionary gatherings,
and every morning at family prayers was careful to invoke a
blessing upon missionary labors. We children were all familiar
with the words of this prayer, which never varied: "We earnestly beseech thee, O God! to give thy special benediction to
all those messengers of the Gospel who carry the glad tidings
of a Saviour's love to the dark and benighted corners of the
earth." When these familiar words came to the ears of the
children of the family they often found us gathered together in
a group in the middle of the room, engaged in anything but
prayer. It was the signal that "Amen" was imminent, and that
it was time to find our way back to our chairs. There, kneeling with our heads to the wall, we buried our faces in our
hands like the older members of the family. It is not very edifying to tell of this; the impression of the prayer, however,
was not altogether lost upon us. We learned to respect the
missionary life as the highest and noblest of vocations.

I had no scruple in attending this convention of Presbyterians with my father. I myself, although I had joined the

Anglican Church, was not at this time very Anglican. I was neither a high-churchman nor a low-churchman. I might more properly have been called an Evangelical.

I remember meeting, about this time, an old college-mate— a Presbyterian, I think—who, after hailing me cordially, said: "I understand, Walworth, that you have become an Episcopalian since we met last." I answered, "Yes." "Well," said he, "are you one of the high heels or low heels?" Not willing to be classed with either faction, I answered that I was not aware of any peculiarity about my heels. "Well," said he, "do you care whether your prayer-books are printed in black letters or red?" "Not at all." My views, in truth, were very broad in regard to Protestantism, and very narrow in respect to Catholicism.

At this annual convention I attended not only all the business meetings of the board, but, as I remember, all the religious services, and did not hesitate to receive communion with the rest.

The principal action of the American Board of Missions at this meeting was one that opened my eyes very much to the practical fruitlessness of Presbyterianism. The standing committee of the board made a public report to the meeting, in which they recommended that thereafter all missionaries sent out to foreign missions should be single and remain unmarried. The reason was that married missionaries have generally large families, which engross much of their time and cripple their capacity for missionary labor. It was found, moreover, that the children of missionaries carried abroad, or born there, were not only deprived of the advantages of a good education, but were exposed to the evil influences of heathen immoralities. This made it necessary to send them home in large numbers to be maintained at the expense of the board. Hence the recommendation of the committee to employ only celibates in foreign missionary labor.

The report of this committee fell like a thunderclap upon the assembled multitude. Here was, in fact, an unexpected justification of the Catholic Church in her enjoining a life of celibacy upon her clergy, and in her employment of so many women vowed to celibacy in Christian education. The agitation of the assembly was intensified by the shock given to a large number of ladies present, wives and daughters both of clergymen and of laymen. These women, indeed, formed a majority of the audience present. Such ladies, I think it may safely be said, are generally more interested in missionary work abroad than are their fathers, brothers, and husbands, and more inclined to be generous in its support.

The report of the committee had cast a wet blanket upon the whole assemblage. A silence prevailed which was ominous.

At this juncture, looking down from the gallery, I saw my father rise on the floor below to address the meeting. He opposed the recommendation of the committee as a most dangerous experiment, and most injurious to the missionary cause. He dwelt particularly upon the value of woman's work and influence in the foreign field. This sentiment prevailed, and the unfortunate report was as promptly and effectually suppressed as the guinea-pig in "Wonderland" when "Alice" sat down upon him. I asked my father afterwards how he could bring himself to make such an argument. The facts presented by the report were manifestly true, I said, and the conclusion to which the committee had come was inevitable. No missionary work could prosper with missionaries so handicapped.

"That's true enough," he replied. "Our foreign missions are doing very little. The expense of supporting the missionaries would be greatly lessened if they would go without families and remain unmarried; but don't you see that in that case we would have no missions at all? Women would not be employed, men would not go, and all the enthusiasm at home about missions would die out; besides little money could be gathered to keep them up. Didn't you see how all life was taken out of the meeting by the reading of that report?"

I said: "Yes. But what is the use of keeping up foreign missions among the heathen when the heathen are not converted?" He admitted the scarcity of converts, but in a moody way said: "The thought of foreign missions helps to keep religion alive at home."

Coming from a lawyer this reply seemed to me very strange and unsatisfactory. It avoided the main issue, and easily admitted of a demurrer. The Presbyterians were thus, to my mind, placed in the position of a body of Christians maintaining a great humbug. And furthermore another question was brought forward to a prominence. If celibacy was practically necessary to missionary work, why not important also to all laborers in the Christian ministry? To admit this was to score a point in favor of clerical celibacy, if not of popery. I was imbued with the prevalent suspicions of horns and hoofs, but from this time forward I felt that in one strong point affecting true Christian life in the church Protestants were far behind.

The opening of the fall term next ensuing of the General Seminary of the Protestant Episcopal Church of New York City found me at Twentieth Street, in my room in the east building. There were two long buildings at that time, each flanked at both ends by dwelling houses for the professors.

The institution to which I was now attached was of a much higher order, both in the character of its professors and the scholarly habits of its students, than any other that I knew of. Bishop Onderdonk, of New York, was its president. He was a high-churchman of the highest type. He was a fearless and tenacious polemic, and strongly inclined in favor of the Oxford movement. He was also professor of ecclesiastical polity. The text-book that he used in class was Hooker, with free use of a work by Law, the non-juror, in all that regarded apostolical succession. His classes were not very frequent nor very regular; but the subject-matter of his lectures and recitations was the all-important one to Episcopalians of apostolical succession, and the divine institution of the clergy in three distinct orders.

Dr. Samuel H. Turner was dean of the faculty, and taught hermeneutics. It would be difficult to define his position as either high or low. He was not what could be called evangelical. He hated cant of all kinds, whether nasal or pompous, and when officiating in the chapel expedited his prayers with the utmost simplicity. The students understood him well, and none of them, I think, attributed his carelessness of manner to a want of earnestness.

Dr. Bird Wilson, professor of systematic divinity (at that time we called it dogmatic theology), stood very high in the opinion of the students, though out of class-time he mingled very little with them. He was the "judicious Hooker" of the seminary. He sailed serenely above all the currents and eddies of party wrangling, like the moon above the clouds. His text-book was *Pearson on the Creed.*

Dr. Ogilby was not a very great man among the faculty, but a very strongly marked one. His branch was ecclesiastical history, in which he succeeded Bishop Whittingham. He was enthusiastically high church, and bitterly opposed to what, in common with the most of his class, he most uncivilly called Romanism, and was scarcely less hostile to Dissenters. Ecclesiastical history to this professor was not so much a field of truth as a forest of materials from which he lopped cudgels for controversy. His very pronunciation was devoutly English.

The professor of pastoral theology was the Rev. Dr. Benjamin I. Haight. He heard us preach our sermons in class, and criticised them. His only text-book, as I remember, was a treatise on pulpit eloquence, by Claude, the celebrated opponent of Bossuet. I owe much to this admirable treatise, and know of nothing to equal it. Dr. Haight was for many years the rector of All Saints' Church, in Henry Street, at the corner of Scannel. He was a man of grave deportment—a *via media* man, safe and cautious, and consequently not over zealous or vigorous.

Among all the officers of the seminary Dr. Clement C. Moore stands forth most distinctly pictured in my memory. He was the author of the famous verses beginning, "'Twas the Night before Christmas." His residence was a fine old mansion fronting the seminary on Twentieth Street, on a large plot of ground with pine-trees. There it was, I am glad to believe, that, as he himself tells us, when

> "Mamma in her 'kerchief and I in my cap
> Had just settled ourselves for a nice winter's nap,"

Santa Claus interrupted him by coming down the chimney with

his pack of gifts. Santa Claus himself could not be more welcome to children than was this odd and genial man upon his
appearance in the Hebrew class. He was very particular in his
ways; but one great feature of his peculiarity was, that he was
utterly unartificial. He was droll, but unconsciously so. He
never joked in the class, but always something made the class-
room seem merry when he was in it. He was a true scholar
in Hebrew. His knowledge of Hebrew words did not seem to
be derived from the dictionary alone. He knew each word
familiarly, and remembered all the different places where it
occurred in the Hebrew Bible, and so could prove its significance in one place by the meaning which necessarily attached
to it elsewhere.

After this brief introduction of the reader to the members of the faculty, I now turn back to my own room with
its surroundings, and to my first impressions of the institution.
The main hall in the east building led from the front, then
on Twentieth Street, to the rear, and was crossed by a lateral
hall somewhat narrower. My room was in the second story on
the west side of the great hall, with windows looking out upon
Twentieth Street. Alfred B. Beach, my room-mate, and I
occupied this apartment as a study-room, and each had a separate sleeping apartment behind and connecting with it. Beach
still lives, and is rector of St. Peter's Church in New York
City.

Across the hall, directly opposite our door, was the room
occupied by Arthur Carey, a memorable young man, whose influence upon my own life has been very great. I shall have
frequent occasion to recur to him in these pages.

On the opposite or west side of my study, and divided from
it by a partition wall, was a room occupied by James A. Mc-
Master, the door of which was reached by the smaller passage
already mentioned. Beach and I were thus flanked in between
two leading spirits of the seminary, widely differing in natural
character, but both far advanced in that current which soon
afterwards carried so many Anglicans into the faith and communion of the ancient church.

McMaster was an old acquaintance whom I had known at

Union College. He entered the freshman class of that institution when I began my junior year, and I remember well the amusement which, as an eccentric lad fresh from the country, he excited amongst his fellow-students. His unusual height, for even at that time he must have been very nearly six-feet-two, his thin face, prominent nose, eagle eye, and impetuous manner made him conspicuous at once among his companions. They soon found out, however, that he was no ever-green, but one born to command respect. His position at the seminary in Twentieth Street was already a well-defined one; and although disliked by many for his aggressiveness, no one ventured to look down upon him.

He was the first to open my eyes to that peculiar atmosphere which all who came to the seminary must necessarily breathe. Some called it Catholic; some called it Romish and superstitious; some called it a spirit of reform, and return to true doctrine and genuine piety; and others regarded it as a relapse into religious darkness and barbarism. Whatever it might be, however, the seminary was recognized by all as the focus of a new religious life in the Episcopalian body. It was not low-churchism, neither was it " high-and-dry."

McMaster entered my room one evening soon after my arrival, and was in conversation with me for an hour or more. He chanced to use the expression of " baptismal regeneration." It was something perfectly new to me, strange though it may seem, for I was now already an Episcopalian of some five years standing. " What do you mean?" said I. " Baptism is simply a ceremony—something outward and visible to the eye. Regeneration, however, is the new birth—a change of the soul into a new life. The two words, therefore, put together signify nothing." My friend, however, insisted that the two words expressed very properly a true Christian doctrine, and one clearly contained in the Holy Scripture. He referred to the baptism of St. Paul, and quoted the words of Ananias: " And now why tarriest thou? Rise up and be baptized, and wash away thy sins." From this text he argued that baptism, duly received, carried with it the pardon of sin, and that the pardon of sin to Saul involved a new birth given to his soul. I doubted the correctness of this citation, and although McMaster looked for it in the New Testament, he was not able at the time to find it.

New as this doctrine of baptismal regeneration was to me, and unconvinced as I remained notwithstanding my friend's argument, the very statement of it fixed itself so firmly in my mind that I remained for a long time sleepless during the night revolving the question, and unable to dismiss it. I took the first opportunity I found to cross the hall into Carey's room and ask him to explain what McMaster had meant.

"I see," said Carey, "that this doctrine appears to you absurd. One thing, however, you will be obliged to acknowledge: that it is the doctrine of the church to which you belong." He then opened the Book of Common Prayer and read to me the words of the baptismal service pronounced by the priest directly after applying the baptismal water to the child, which run as follows: "Seeing, therefore, that this child is now regenerate, etc." He then read to me also the passage from the Acts of the Apostles, which McMaster had not been able to find, in which the Apostle Paul gives to the people an account of his conversion and baptism. And we conversed together a long while on this subject. I was not convinced at once, for the idea of grace conveyed to the soul by means of a sacramental ceremony is something utterly inconsistent with the ordinary training of a Protestant mind. I could not, however, dismiss it from mine, and it was not very long before I received it undoubtingly and with a firmness of conviction which could never afterwards be shaken. It was the entering wedge of a new faith, far broader and deeper than any I then conceived of as possible.

A very interesting and valuable society had been organized amongst the students for the discussion of theological and other questions belonging especially to the clerical profession. Arthur Carey presided over it at that time, and its debates were well attended by all the prominent students of every shade of opinion, puseyites, evangelicals, and independents, high-churchmen, low-churchmen, and no churchmen-at-all, all gathered together to maintain their distinctive views. I was attracted to one of these meetings soon after my arrival at the seminary, and the

debate which took place opened before me a new world of
surprise.   The question as debated turned chiefly upon this
point : Whether Protestants, congregated in folds not covered by
the Apostolic Succession, were Christians.   I was amazed to
find that a very strong array of speakers, if not indeed the prevailing sentiment, was unfavorable to dissenters as forming a
part of Christendom.   In all my experience I had hitherto never
heard such a point raised.   I was shocked as well as amazed,
and before the debate closed I took occasion to rise and express my wonder.   I was too young in theology to make the
necessary distinctions which belong to such a question.   I used
only the *argumentum ad verecundiam.*   I said that I was the
child of Presbyterian parents and that I recognized several of
the speakers as having been brought up in that denomination.
I thought that some of the opinions expressed there so strongly
and freely would sound very strangely at the firesides from
which they had come.   I acknowledged my inability to deal
with the question very logically, but I felt sure that there was
a mistake somewhere.   Some apologetic explanations were then
made for my benefit by the speakers whose remarks had surprised me, but they failed to give me any new light or diminish
my wonder.

Carey, the president, was the last speaker.   It was his part
to sum up the debate, and he did it with a power, a gentleness,
a thoughtfulness, and discrimination, which were characteristic of
himself and marvellous in one so young.   He drew distinctions in
defining the words " Church " and " Christian " not very unlike
such as would be drawn by a Catholic " to the manner born."
His doctrine was all on the High-Church side, and gave no
countenance to what is known as Evangelical Protestantism ;
but there was no wounding in his words, they had in them no
personal sting, though some of the speakers must have felt gently
rebuked by them.   I conceived a strong admiration and love
for the young man which has never left me since.   One evening, shortly after this debate, I was sitting alone in my room
when Carey entered.   I was unoccupied.   I could not read
evenings, for my sight had begun to fail—a trouble which, dating
from that time, has followed me with variations during my

whole life. Carey expressed his sympathy at the condition of my sight, and asked if I would not like to have him read to me. I accepted his offer eagerly. He took up a copy of the New Testament which lay upon my table and commenced reading from the Gospel of St. John, opening at the fourteenth chapter and reading through to the end. I had never before then appreciated so fully the solemn beauty of the Holy Scriptures. Carey was an admirable reader, keeping midway between a tedious monotony and all extravagance of expression. His voice was low and sweet, and had a quietness of suppressed feeling in its tones which was magnetic. He made no comments on anything he read, but let the sacred page tell its own story. I never read those chapters now, particularly the three containing our Lord's discourse after the Last Supper, but my thoughts go back to that memorable evening, and I see Carey's kindly face before me and his hair glowing like gold in the lamp-light. His influence over me was at once established, and I thank God for it still.

McMaster was a man of a very different mould from Arthur Carey, although perhaps the most intimate friend that he had at the seminary. He also exercised a strong influence in the movement towards Catholicism. If he did not bring down much game, he was very effective in starting it, and was always ready for a discussion.

One day Harwood, a student belonging to an advanced class, was visiting my room-mate and myself, and broached some opinions which Beach, a staunch high-churchman, looked upon as unsound. Neither he nor I could maintain any discussion with a student of Harwood's experience. Beach was glad to call in reinforcements. He had heard the step of McMaster passing along the hall on his way to descend the stairs. Going quickly to the door, Beach called him back, saying, "Stop, Mac, I want you! Here's Harwood. He says the Ecumenical Councils are not infallible." McMaster turned back at once. He strode into the room and, throwing his long leg over the back of a chair and resting his arm upon his knee, he fixed his eagle eyes upon Harwood and vociferated: "Where are your grounds?" Harwood was not a man to be alarmed, and immediately a hot discussion ensued which lasted until both parties had expended their ammunition. Beach and I remained prudently silent.

I was not a classmate of McMaster's, being in my first year when he was in his third, and can give very little account of him in regard to his proficiency in the regular studies of a seminary course. He was certainly a great reader and was very fond of reading rare books, especially books by Catholic authors, or of old fashioned Anglican divines, little known to Episcopalians of the present day. The library of the institution afforded many notable books of either class. Among these I remember the *Summa* of St. Thomas Aquinas and the *Catena Aurea*. These furnished him with an artillery of heavy guns very formidable in controversy. While busily occupied in his room one day with a volume of St. Thomas on the table before him, he was interrupted by a sudden rap at the door. Knowing it to be locked, and not caring to be interrupted, he made no answer; the knock was repeated, to as little purpose. The knocking still continued, and, it becoming evident that some one was there who believed him to be in and was determined to get admission, he turned his eyes towards the door and saw above it, looking down upon him through the transom, the face of his brother, a Presbyterian clergyman. This brother was as tall as himself, and the door was no screen between them. Seclusion was now hopeless. Our mediæval student was obliged to turn his attention from the Angelic Doctor to Dr. McMaster, of Ballston Spa.

James A. McMaster will, no doubt, figure for a long while in the history of Catholic progress in this country as a prominent actor. It is probable that some friend—better acquainted with the events of his later life—will write his biography as it should be written, with care and study. I must, therefore, be pardoned if I pass over the more serious events of his career, and more valuable traits of his character, and endeavor to place him before the reader in such strong lights and shadows, and such colors, as to present a lively picture of the man, but not an analytical study.

I may as well say here that I found myself occupying a somewhat anomalous position among the students of the General Seminary. I was no churchman, either high or low ; I had taken no interest in the Oxford movement, and had very little conception of what it was. The accidental circumstance, while studying law at Canandaigua, of boarding and lodging nearly opposite an Episcopalian church, and of having its organist for a fellow-lodger, had led me to join its choir and attend its services. This I continued afterwards by mere habit until 1839, when I received confirmation at the hands of Bishop Onderdonk at St. Paul's Church, Albany. I was at that time prosecuting my law studies in the office of Stevens & Cagger, of that city. Dr. Kip, afterwards Bishop of California, was at that time rector of St. Paul's, and I had become a singer in his choir and the superintendent of his Sunday-school. No questions had been put to me as to what I believed or did not believe. I found myself in the Anglican Church with apparently the full liberty to believe what I liked and to change my belief unquestioned. I had, no doubt, some very strong religious convictions, which I think I would have maintained at the cost of my life ; but with these convictions I could without scruple have become a Presbyterian or Methodist as readily as an Episcopalian. Such a man cannot be classed as a churchman. I do not think I could very properly have been styled an Evangelical. In the matter of "justification by faith only" I was scarcely a staunch Protestant. That doctrine seemed to me Antinomian, and consequently immoral. I knew that many Protestants acquiesced in it who did not practically rely upon it, but I would have been unwilling to profess it in any distinct language if this had been exacted of me.

Under these circumstances it can easily be understood that I had no bias which kept me from associating freely and intimately with any student, whether dryly high or evangelically low, ritualistic, puseyite, or of still stronger Romanizing tendencies. I readily formed friendships with any one, whether in or out of the seminary, in whose personality I saw the measure of a well-made man. Among my most familiar associates was my cousin, Charles Platt, who was one year in advance of me. He was the son of Commodore Charles Platt, of the United States navy, and a candidate of our western diocese.

In that same class were to be numbered William Everett, who had commenced life as a medical doctor and is now pastor of the Church of the Nativity in Second Avenue. New York City. Harwood was a prominent member of the same class; in hermeneutics, ecclesiastical history, and in almost everything else, holding to German notions, a high churchman in matters of authority and externals, but rather low-church in doctrine. Harwood is still living, holding the rectorship of Trinity Church, New Haven, Conn.

Mason Gallagher was also in Platt's class, and a candidate of Bishop De Lancey's; he is still living, I am told, and is now a preacher among the reformed Episcopalians. He was an Irishman, perhaps an Orangeman, of the controversial stamp. I remember little of his polemics, however, except that I frequently saw him in the gymnasium. We had a room in the seminary appropriated to gymnastics, with parallel bars, poles and ropes for climbing and swinging, boxing-gloves, etc. This room was much frequented by Gallagher, as also by Wyatt, a very gentlemanly and superior young man, son of Dr. Wyatt, rector of St. Paul's Church in Charles Street, Baltimore. These two I often saw engaged in pounding each other with boxing-gloves. I remember little else of Wyatt, but shall have occasion to speak of Gallagher again. In the same class was a Greek from Greece proper, if I remember right, named Stamos Trikaliotes. His classmates remember somewhat vividly how he preached a sermon, as an exercise in Dr. Haight's department, in which some curious chemical statements convulsed both the doctor and the whole class with laughter. He was, when I knew him, no Greek in belief. He was sufficiently Evangelical in his notions to satisfy even one so profoundly Protestant as Bishop McIlvain, of Ohio.

A leading and cultivated mind also in Platt's class was Benjamin F. Whicher, who died recently a Catholic layman Harry Montgomery, afterwards familiar to New-Yorkers as Episcopalian pastor of a church in their city, was, as a student, very enthusiastic in matters of rite, and ceremony, and ecclesiastical art. Gardner of Maine, a very companionable man, was in my class, and a fondness for the same studies helped to make our friendship more familiar. Geer was our organist and choir-master, and as I met him constantly at practice and sat next to him in chapel, I have him in very distinct remembrance. Some other faces come back to me vividly enough, whose names I find it impossible to recall. Wadhams, Mc-Vicker, Donelly, Gibson, and other of my familiar associates, were all deeply interested in the Oxford movement, and not much afraid of Rome.

Carey and McMaster can scarcely be classed with these, for their hearts already looked lovingly and earnestly towards the ancient faith, and I am persuaded that nothing but the example of Newman, Oakeley, and others who were their acknowledged masters, kept them back from the arms of the church. Among the Evangelicals in the seminary I found none that attracted me. I had some friends of this kind, however, in the city. My sister, Mrs. Jenkins, lived in Eleventh Street near Fifth Avenue. Mrs. Codwise, a Presbyterian lady who lived in St. Mark's Place, Eighth Street, was an old family friend. From the first moment of my arrival at the seminary she kept watch and ward over me, suspected me of hair-shirts, crosses and crucifixes, and sought to introduce me into a circle of Evangelicals, Episcopalians or otherwise. As I frequently took tea at her house and spent the evening with her, I met a variety of clergymen of every possible kind. Each one of these she took care to assure me was eminent, interesting, and lovely. Now and then among them appeared some man of note that might be called eminent if not interesting. Dr. Cummings, of the Church of the Puritans and a noted anti-popery preacher, was one of these. I found him very talkative, very bitter, and most unlovable. I went with her one evening to hear him preach; I never heard such bitterness, hatred, and bigotry concentrated into one sermon. "Isn't he fervent? isn't he charming?" said the good lady as we went out. I fear that my reply shocked her more than the denunciations of the minister had done. Most of the divines that I met at her house seemed to me sufficiently dull and dry. I valued the good lady herself above a thousand of them.

One evening, at her earnest solicitation, I accompanied her to the museum on the corner of Broadway and Chambers Street. She had been reading about Indian missions and this made her anxious to witness an Indian war-dance. We started early in order to pay a visit first to the Bible Society. Passing through one of the rooms she stopped me suddenly before a large arm-chair.

"Look at that!" said she. "What do you think that is?"

"I see nothing," I replied, "but an arm-chair. I remember one in my grandmother's kitchen very like it."

"No," she said, "it is something more than that. You'll be delighted when I tell you. I want you to sit down in it." I complied.

"Now then, my dear young friend," she exclaimed, "I want you to understand that you are sitting in the very chair that the 'Dairyman's Daughter' died in. Think of it! How do you feel now?"

"Mrs. Codwise," said I solemnly, "I am astonished that a Protestant lady so noted for true piety and horror of superstition should endeavor to teach me the veneration of relics."

"Oh, how provoking you are!" she exclaimed. "Is it possible that you can sit in that chair—that chair—that chair! and not be thrilled with emotion?"

Our visit to the museum was not more successful. I enjoyed the war-dance very much, but the good lady was nearly frightened out of her senses by the ferocity of the painted warriors, who were true Indians, and the terrible ring of their war-whoops.

"O let us go! take me away!" she said. "I can't endure it. I shall die. This is dreadful." I stood up and looked around upon the crowd. It was impossible to make our way out, and I told her so. She closed her eyes and endeavored to deafen her ears, and so wait for the termination of the exhibition. I presume that her interest in the Indian missions continued, but am confident that nothing thereafter could have induced her to become a missionary. In truth, so far as may be judged by the injudicious measures she took to lead my soul in the right way, she had little vocation for the missionary life.

The great doctrinal bulwark of the Anglican system is well understood to be its claim to Apostolical Succession. One can scarcely claim to be distinctly Episcopalian until he has learned that. I had not yet learned it when I arrived at the seminary, and attached little importance to it. It did not come up in the seminary course until the second year. I mastered pretty well what there was of it in my first year. It was brought out prominently before the New York public in the famous Potts and Wainwright controversy, which originated as follows:

Rufus Choate, the great Boston lawyer and orator, made an address that year in New York City at the celebration of the landing of the Pilgrims at Plymouth. In the course of his address he spoke of the Pilgrim fathers as having founded "a church without a bishop and a state without a king." This had occasioned considerable merriment in the audience. Dr. Wainwright, of New York, occupied a chair upon the stage and near the speaker. At the dinner which followed, Dr. Wainwright, when rising to compliment the orator, took occasion to parry the joke by saying that "while a state could very well exist without a king, there could be no church without a bishop." Dr. Potts, the pastor of a fashionable Presbyterian church on Fifth Avenue, took umbrage at this declaration and opened a controversy with Dr. Wainwright in the public papers. The arguments for and against the necessity of a succession of bishops to constitute a church, and for and against the claim of Episcopalians to such a succession, were pretty thoroughly discussed in the debate.

Being a greenhorn in theology, I followed this discussion with much attention. So did Hiram Walworth, an uncle of mine who resided in Hudson Square. I frequently spent my evenings at his house, and we took pleasure in reading and canvassing the points of this controversy. The necessity of a distinctive order of bishops to constitute a valid Christian church soon became quite manifest to me, though my uncle would not admit it. His objections, however, were always shrewd and forcibly put, and converted what might have been a superficial reading into a careful study. I thus became for the first time a veritable Episcopalian.

It may not be amiss in this place to add a few more words in regard to this uncle.

His family were Presbyterians, and he loved to profess himself as a thorough Calvinist.   He was a great joker, and this
profession was one of his favorite jokes.   He loved to put forward the most hideous tenets of Calvinism in their worst form.
He held a pew in a Presbyterian church near by, but he did
not think it important to attend its services with the rest of
his family.   When I ventured cautiously to rebuke him for this
he would say:

"What should I go to church for?   I know well enough all
the minister could tell me."

"You ought to go there in order to pray."

"What do I want to pray for?   It's his duty, and let him
attend to it."

"Yes, my dear uncle," I insisted, "but you need to pray
yourself, and maintain the spirit of prayer in your soul in order
to save it."

"No, I don't.   I'm elected."

"Don't be too certain of that, uncle.   You need to make
your vocation and election sure."

"Why, it is sure already.   Don't you know that full assur-
ance is given to the elect?"

My aunt would often interrupt the conversation with her
remonstrances, but it was a merry thing for him to make fun of
us both.

I had also a married sister living in New York, whose residence was on Eleventh Street, as already stated.   I took my
meals at her house for some time at the commencement of my
course, and often spent my evenings there.   She endeavored to
keep me safe against the dangerous influences of the seminary,
and was very glad to read to me such books as she thought
salutary.   One of these was D'Aubigny's *History of the Reformation.*   No one book ever did so much to alienate me from Protestantism.   If it had been written by a Catholic, I should have
distrusted it; but it was written by a Protestant, a devout ad-
mirer of Luther; one who looked upon him as above all others
the great leader of that revolution, and divinely sent to begin
and carry on the movement.   I had been brought up to look
upon him in the same light.   To my sight he had always been

a man of saintly character and a hero. D`Aubigny keeps back much of the vulgar self-indulgence attributed to Luther by other authors, as well as the coarse and gross language which appears in some of his works. But his Luther is no hero. He is simply a religious and political agitator. To my mind he is as much marked by duplicity as by audacity. I do not conceive how any unprejudiced and thoughtful man, when listening to this history, could borrow the words of the Evangelist and say of this great heresiarch : *There was a man sent from God whose name was Martin Luther.* I felt that I had been imposed upon. The scales dropped from my eyes. I saw Dagon fall to pieces in his own temple. To my sister's great surprise I frequently interrupted her reading by saying : " What sort of a hero is that ? Can a worshipper of Luther make nothing better of him ? " I expressed my surprise in a very similar way to Arthur Carey. " I have had enough of Luther," said I. He answered after his quiet manner : " You would probably like Melanchthon better. He is at least more of a scholar—more refined and gentle."

About the same time I encountered an early acquaintance on the ferry-boat to Staten Island. He was loud in his denunciations, not only of Luther, Melanchthon, Calvin, and other reformers, but declaimed violently against every sect of Christians. " Through their false doctrines and hypocrisy they are demoralizing the world more and more every day." " What benefit, then," I inquired, " has the Reformation been to the world ? " He was staggered for a moment, but replied : " Well, it was something at least for religion to get rid of her old rags." He was evidently on his way towards infidelity. On the contrary, I was more hopeful than ever. Only old clouds of ignorance and prejudice were disappearing; new light was breaking; and I felt that I had never parted with any point of Christian teaching that was positive and of a nature to be called faith.

I had now so far got to be an Episcopalian as to prefer it before any other church, and for positive reasons. This made me feel quite at home at the seminary. In the next chapter I will endeavor to give some idea of class-life there.

CHAPTER II.

A FAVORITE class with many of the students at the Chelsea Seminary was that over which Dr. Clement C. Moore presided—the Hebrew class.   There was no study to which my chum Beach and I devoted ourselves with more perseverance and regularity.

In the annals of the Chelsea Seminary Dr. Moore will not figure merely as professor of Hebrew.   He was a prominent patron of the institution, and was closely identified with all its interests.   Its very location on Twentieth Street, opposite to his own residence and between the Ninth and Tenth Avenues, was a thing of his selection and due to his choice.   He taught in the seminary for thirty years previous to 1850, at which time he retired from active service as professor emeritus.   In 1821 he was made professor of Biblical learning.   His second appointment was to teach Oriental and Greek literature.   He was the author of a " Hebrew and Greek Lexicon," in two volumes, published in 1809, and other works.   It is a strange thing that a man of such great and varied learning as Dr. Moore, so versed in oriental and classic literature and a pioneer in matters of rare and deep research, should only be known to the general world of readers by one single ballad, "The Visit of St. Nicholas."   A volume of poems, his only published work of this kind, was given to the public in 1844, while I was still a seminarian.   This volume contains among other things some verses accompanying a gift of flowers to a friend.   That friend, Mr. P. Hone, returned an answer also in verse, which so well specifies the various accomplishments of the worthy professor that I need only to give it to the reader in order to furnish a picture of this notable man :

FRONT VIEW WEST BUILDING OLD EPISCOPALIAN SEMINARY, CHELSEA SQUARE, NEW YORK.

" Filled as thou art with Attic fire,
      And skilled in classic lore divine,
Not yet content, wouldst thou aspire
      In Flora's gorgeous wreath to shine?
Wouldst thou in language of the rose
      Lessons of wisdom seek t' impart,
Or in the violet's breath disclose
      The feelings of a generous heart?
Come as thou wilt, my warm regard
      And welcome shall thy steps attend;
Scholar, musician, florist, bard—
      More dear to me than all, as friend.
Bring flowers and poesy, a goodly store,
      Like Dickens' Oliver—I ask for *Moore.*"

The principal object of our studies in Hebrew was to prepare us for the class in hermeneutics over which Dr. Samuel
H. Turner presided. After reading the first two or three chapters of Genesis, our readings in the Hebrew Testament were
confined to its Messianic parts. These parts were always carefully marked out for the Hebrew class by Dr. Turner himself.
Dr. Moore confined his teaching strictly to the Hebrew, and
the translation of the parts thus marked out, but never med-
dled with the interpretation of Scripture. The nearest that he
ever came to this in dealing with our class was one day when
we were translating the seventeenth verse of the twenty-first
Psalm, which, in the Septuagint and in the Vulgate and other
Christian versions, reads, "They have dug (or pierced) my hands
and feet." When we came to these words, the student whose
turn it was translated the passage as above. "Well, yes," said
Dr. Moore, "that's the way we read it in our English Bible,
but here in this Hebrew Bible we have *Kari*, which would
oblige us to translate the passage as the Jews do, 'Like a lion,
my hands and feet.' To be sure, that don't seem to make good
sense; but that is no business of mine. I am not here to
inculcate good sense, but to teach Hebrew. Some learned people will tell you that the rabbins have changed the text on
purpose. Well, perhaps they did. I didn't. Or, when you

come to Dr. Turner's class, perhaps he will tell you that the word got changed by careless writing in Hebrew, shortening the tail of the last letter till they turned the *vau* into a *yod*. That would change *Karu* into *Kari*. In that case, all we need to make it right is to put the long tail on again. Then we have *Karu*, and can translate the passage, 'They pierced my hands and my feet.' Well, well, well! Let them fix it their own way. That's none of my business. Here we have *Kari*, and that means 'Like a lion.' In my class, young man, you'll have to read it that way. I don't bother myself much about old versions, nor old manuscripts, nor old commentators, nor old rabbins. I am only a layman, but I know what Hebrew is when I see it in the book before us. Humph! Go on.'"

I have already said that the Hebrew class was a great favorite with me as with many others, and what we learned there was of the greatest advantage when dealing with Dr. Turner in the interpretation of Scripture. I have lost some valuable books in my day, sometimes through lending, sometimes through the casualties of house-cleaning, and sometimes because an eventful life has forced me to forsake them. For none of these have I mourned so much as for the Hebrew Bible which I interlined most carefully, in my study-room, with equivalent English words of the good doctor's rendering. I have never been able to recover it.

My reminiscences of this seminary are largely made up of scenes from Professor Turner's class-room. I seem to see the professor before me now. I can still recall him most vividly, as he then sat at his desk. He was devoted to his class. His earnest devotion showed itself in his eyes, brows, mouth, nose, and in his very hair, as he gazed upon the Greek Testament before him, or bent his looks upon us to gather in from the expression of our faces the effect of his criticisms. We could see his legs under the desk. There his little hands took a busy part in the exegesis, pinching his trousers at the knees. One foot or the other was always tapping the floor of the platform. His feet were very small. This we could see for ourselves, and I knew from his shoemaker that he was very particular about his shoes.

All this liveliness on the part of Professor Turner was perfectly unaffected. Indeed, there was something about him that
always seemed to protest against affectation of every kind.
When it was his turn to preside at the morning service in the
chapel, he protested against that deep-mouthed throttling of the
words of the service so frequent amongst his brethren of the
clergy. He carried this even to an excess. In his dislike of
pomposity he actually danced over very solemn words. He
always chose the short absolution, and made very short work
of it, too. On the contrary, when reading the lessons from
Holy Scripture, he gave a triumphant and jerky emphasis to
certain inelegant words of the text which others are apt to skip
over lightly, through a sense of delicacy.

Professor Turner had a strong predilection for those students who showed a particular interest in his class, and this
without exacting any strict adherence to his own interpreta-
tions. Indeed, there were some of us that took a quiet
pleasure in hunting up authorities which militated with his
views. He never manifested any offence at this. Some dialogue
like the following would then take place :

" Well, have you any authority for that interpretation ? "

" Yes, sir ; I find Theodoret quoted for it."

" Ah, indeed, Theodoret ! Well, I don't wish to dispute that
Theodoret is an authority, but I must beg leave to differ with
Theodoret in this case. Does Theodoret or the commentator
who quotes him assign any reasons for their opinion ? "

The reasons being given, the doctor would then continue:
" The authority, no doubt, is highly respectable. I wish I could
say as much for the reasons assigned." The doctor would then
carefully go over the ground a second time, without offering
the least rebuke to the independence of the student, and without saying anything to discourage free study, even though
dissenters should be consulted or Catholic authors.

I was one of those who loved to ramble in study of authorities, especially after my first year, when I had found out that
the world of theological doctrine was broader and deeper than
I had ever dreamed of before. I was even bold enough on one
occasion to give a translation to the Greek text differing in

several respects from the King James version. The passage is that of Hebrews vi. 4, 5, 6. To the surprise of the whole class, I translated this passage as follows:

'For it is impossible for those, who were once enlightened, etc., etc., and are fallen away, to be renewed again *by penance.*"

After hesitating a moment, the professor said quietly: " I don't object, Mr. Walworth, to your reversing of the sequence in this passage, nor your changing the voice of the verb, nor to your using the word penance, which may very well be understood as meaning nothing else than repentance; but how can 'by penance' be given as a correct translation of *'eis metanoian'?* *Eis* is a preposition, and is equivalent to *unto* and *into*, in English. I do not know of a single instance where any dictionary or translator has given it the sense of *by*. Do you?"

I had anticipated this objection, and it was my good luck to be furnished with one instance in the English Testament itself. It was easy for the good doctor to dispose of this point in my case. I had little confidence in it and was only amusing myself. What struck me most at the time was the gentleness, equanimity, and even respect, with which he treated my presumption.

I did not get off so easily with another friend, who took it much to heart. In our class was a student from Maine named Gardner, who was not only a good scholar but very fond of hermeneutics, and of all close and nice study in language. He was, moreover, a sincere Protestant, albeit of the high-church stamp. Having occasion to visit his room that same day, he received me with a seriousness that was startling.

"What is the matter, Gardner?" I inquired. " Have you received any ill news?"

"O Walworth!" said he, "I didn't think you'd do it. I didn't think you'd do it!"

"Why, what have I done?"

"I have been anxious about you," he answered, "but I never thought it would come to this."

"There must be something dreadful in your mind, Gardner. What is it? What have I done?"

"I did not think you would give such a translation to *metanoian—penance.* Oh! It is too bad; how could you do it?"

"Well," I said, "under all the circumstances, it was a fool-ish thing. Since it grieves you so much I take it back. Come, my dear fellow, forgive me, and brighten up again."

But poor Gardner could not be pacified.

"You'll end in Rome yet, Walworth," he said: "you'll end in Rome."

It seemed to me at one time that Gardner himself was dan-gerously near the jaws of the same great dragon. He was very nearly led into the doctrine of transubstantiation by a learned work of Dr. Wiseman on that subject. His arguments, derived from a critical examination of the sixth chapter of St. John and from St. Paul's First Epistle to the Corinthians (x. 16 and xi. 24–29), seemed to me to be very strong. What struck Gard-ner's mind most forcibly, however, was the immense learning displayed by Dr. Wiseman to show that the words used by our Lord in instituting the Blessed Sacrament, "This is my body. This is my blood," must necessarily be understood literally. The force of the context, the circumstances attending the insti-tution of the Eucharist, and the comparison of various passages referring to the Eucharist before and after its institution, these arguments would seem strong enough to convince any mind that fairly gives its attention to them. Gardner's fond-ness for critical learning, however, made him attach much greater importance to the almost infinite variety of citations from au-thors in almost every language to show the uses of the verb *einai*, when it is used literally and when it must be understood figuratively. I soon grew tired of all this learned detail, the most of which seemed to me trivial. Gardner, however, was both attracted and alarmed by it. He carried these questions to Dr. Turner, who entered into them with full sympathy. Gard-ner became at last convinced that the saddle-bags were as full on the Anglican side of the horse as the other, and he got no nearer to Romanism.

I think I caused some considerable chagrin to Professor Turner on another occasion when he was anxious to show off his class at examination. I was called upon to explain the sense of our Lord's words in "the sermon on the mount" where, according to King James's version, he says to his disci-

ples: "If thy right eye offend thee, pluck it out. . . . And
if thy right hand offend thee, cut it off." I interpreted the
passage as applying to an occasion of sin where the dangerous
temptation is so great that there is no reasonable hope of escap-
ing from sin except by putting away the occasion or flying from
it. The doctor was well satisfied with this, but unfortunately
carried the matter a little too far by asking me if our Lord by
this teaching ever intended that one should actually pluck out
an eye or cut off an arm. I answered that I thought the ur-
gency of the occasion might sometimes require such extreme
measures, if there was no other way of keeping in the grace of
God. The doctor was evidently much mortified, as some very
notable clergymen were present at the examination. I had,
moreover, been the very one to handle this passage at a previous class recitation; I had extended its meaning with the
same literal severity, and the doctor had set me right very carefully. He therefore counted on me to do him credit before the
visiting examiners. His brows gathered with vexation, but he
contented himself with setting me right once more. I was sorry
to have grieved him, but I really believed that in such extreme
cases as I had proposed one could dispense with an eye or a
leg, and even lend a hand to getting rid of them. I do not
give this incident in order to fix any interpretation upon the
passage in question, but only to illustrate the professor's gentleness to his pupils, especially to those who took any special interest in his class.

At times the doctor could be petulant enough. During the
Christmas vacation at the close of the year 1843 several students remained at the seminary, including myself and Whicher,
also a candidate from our western diocese. Some of us undertook to decorate the chapel for Christmas. We introduced
evergreens after the usual manner, and as profusely as circumstances would allow, especially around the little chancel. Unfortunately, however, none of us being low-churchmen or evangelical, and none having any great fear of Rome before our
eyes, we introduced a large evergreen cross at the centre of the
chancel railing and directly in front of the desk. Professor
Turner, who was also dean of the faculty, having charge of the

buildings and all the rooms, was either offended at this, or
feared that others would take offence. He sent for Whicher,
berated him soundly, and ordered that the cross should be taken
down. Whicher was disposed to resist this order as being unfriendly to the very symbol of our salvation, and fanatically
evangelical. He consulted with his copartners in misdemeanor,
who encouraged him to carry the case to Bishop Onderdonk,
president of the seminary. This he did. Dr. Onderdonk expressed great surprise at the dean's order, which he considered
very foolish and unnecessary. He advised, however, that we
should submit promptly and quietly to the dean, who was acting strictly in the line of his office and ought to be obeyed.
This ended the matter, but left us feeling very foolish. Episcopalians are not so skittish now. Ritualism has taught them to
face everything Catholic except good doctrine. They are prepared to put on all the robes of popery with the understanding
that nothing serious is meant by it.

It was not very often that anything took place in the class-
rooms to invite controversial discussions. Dr. Wilson, who presided over the department of dogmatic theology, was a truly
learned man, and what would be called a very sound man by
all except ranting evangelicals of the Bishop McIlvaine stamp.
To Dr. Wilson, and to the excellent text-book upon which he
grounded himself, I owe a great deal of instruction in fundamental doctrines of Christianity, which I shall always hold as
very precious. Of course I came to the seminary receiving with
implicit faith the Christian doctrine of the Incarnation. Moreover, I thought that I understood it pretty well. In this, however, I was mistaken. I found that my knowledge of this doctrine was very superficial. This, I believe, is true of almost all
Protestant laymen, and indeed of many of the clergy.

My course in Dr. Wilson's class was never completed, but
yet I learned there a great deal concerning the two-fold nature
of Christ, which helped me forward in that way toward the
true and only church which I was following, unconsciously indeed and slowly, but none the less surely. The Sacrifice of the
Eucharist was not taught in that class as Catholics understand
it—a memorial Sacrifice actually and visibly taking place before

their senses; but the perpetual presence of Christ at the throne of his Father as a victim, and so continuing and perpetuating his sacrifice on Mount Calvary, was so vividly presented to my mind that the Catholic Mass, with all its reality and sacredness, became something easy to receive. Then come in the solemn words of our Lord on the first Holy Thursday, "Do this in commemoration of me." Thus the sacrifice of Christ ceases to be regarded merely as a thing of finished and accomplished history. It is something still going on. Although Christ dies no more, although the actual death scene can only be repeated as a sacred drama, yet that sacred drama is repeated as a divine institution, with a victim present and an offering; it is a visible sacrament with a grace attached to it. It becomes easy now to take in the thought that the great Sacrament is not only

LIFE AT CHELSEA SEMINARY.—"ONE OF THEM."

perpetuated at a celestial altar in the immediate presence of God, but here also amongst us for whose benefit the sacrifice is made. It becomes a part of our worship, indeed the greatest and most solemn act of worship which we can offer. The thoughtful mind makes progress in this way from a mere matter of communions consisting at best only of thoughtful meditations, to a realization of the Catholic Sacrifice of the Mass. The Hebrews had their altar, but the victims offered at that al-

tar were only types of the true victim who was not present;
but Christ our pasch is sacrificed for us, and therefore we keep
the feast. We also, as the apostle says, " have an altar, whereof
they have no power to eat who serve the tabernacle."

Professor Wilson's class and *Pearson on the Creed* came to
me late in my seminary course, but when they did come they
did much for me. They did much to help me forward in my
struggle for a sure and full faith, far more than noisier and
more exciting disputations out of class. They did more for me
also than the less solid but more controversial manner in which
our course of ecclesiastical history was conducted.

Professor Ogilby was a partisan scholar, a controversialist of
the *via media* school. To his mind truth was something which
always poised itself skilfully on a medium line, and at a safe
distance from Rome on the one side and ultra Protestantism on
the other. Adapting all his learning to this *via media*, as a
good strategic point to fight from, he dealt out vigorous blows
to the right and to the left. It was difficult to say which foes
he disliked the most, Catholics or dissenters. If he did not
teach much accurate truth, at least he stirred up many questions of historical importance, which his students could study
up and discuss outside of the class-room.

A little while before I entered the seminary he had been
party to a discussion with Dr. McVickar, of Columbia College, on
the validity of lay baptism. Dr. McVickar maintained the
validity of baptism by laymen, which Professor Ogilby denied.
It was one of the first questions which I encountered upon my
entry into the seminary, and it was some considerable time before I arrived at any settled conviction upon the point. It was
with me a very practical point, for I had been baptized in infancy by a Presbyterian minister; and according to the belief
of Dr. Ogilby and a large part of the Anglican clergy, these
and other dissenting ministers are laymen, having no valid orders. I made up my mind very early to put the validity of
my baptism beyond all doubt, by getting myself baptized again.
I selected as the minister of this new baptism the Rev. Caleb
Clapp, an alumnus of 1839, and an old friend of mine in Saratoga, where he married his wife, but at the time officiating in

New York as rector of Nativity Church, near the East River. I was the superintendent of his Sunday-school, and he entered readily into my views. I reasoned that on the supposition of my first baptism being deficient, no Catholic would ever dispute the validity of this new one on the ground of a want of intention on the part of the minister, since Mr. Clapp was a firm believer in the necessity of baptism, and would not administer it thoughtlessly. Episcopalians could find no fault with a baptism administered by Mr. Clapp, since they could not class him as a layman. Baptists could not object to it on the ground of my being an infant and so incapable of receiving it. And lastly neither Baptists nor schismatic Greeks could object to it, since the method of trine immersion was carefully used. I find the certificate of this baptism securely laid away in a package of diplomas, certificates, and other like papers. It is carefully written out on vellum in my own hand, with the exception of the date and signature. Some of the most significant words are heavily done in imitation of Old English lettering, ornamentally shaded with red. It runs as follows:

"I hereby certify that CLARENCE WALWORTH was by me baptized into the Church of Christ 'in the Name of the FATHER and of the SON and of the HOLY GHOST,' according to the mode of 'trine immersion,' on Thursday, the 22d day of June, in the year of our Redemption One Thousand Eight Hundred and Forty-three. CALEB CLAPP,
Rector of the Church of the Nativity in the city and diocese of New York."

I introduce this event of a second baptism with all its particularity because it shows how a neophyte naturally felt bound to entrench himself in a seminary where so many conflicting opinions made the air hot and lively. Some two years later when received into the true fold by Father Gabriel Rumpler, C.SS.R., rector of the Church of the Holy Redeemer in Third Street, New York, I showed him this certificate. He laughed heartily, and said that this made my baptism about as sure as sure could be, and that I need never trouble myself about it again. Indeed, I never knew its validity to be disputed except by an old priest who wished to have a little fun. He ventured to throw some doubt upon my being a true sheep of the fold yet, for want of salt. I answered that my baptism had taken place in New York Bay, which is sea-water and well salted. He insisted that this salt had not been blessed, and besides that the rite used was insufficient for want of the exorcisms.

"Come to me," said he, "and I will give you the real thing with all the good old ceremonies that your minister omitted. I will give you the true *sal sapientiæ* and drive the devil out for good."

Caleb Clapp, the dear old friend who baptized me in the waters of the ocean with such scrupulous care, died in 1878. He clung to his old parish of the Nativity. I never had the pleasure to welcome him into the visible body of the true church. That he always belonged to the soul of that church I never doubted, nor that he now rests in the true fold.

My rebaptism by an Episcopalian minister is by no means a thing so very rare. Episcopalian clergymen generally hold that baptism is a necessary sacrament, or at least a ceremony of very high importance. Another prevailing opinion among them is that all dissenting ministers who have not received ordination from some bishop whose orders have come down to him regularly, according to the law of uninterrupted apostolical succession, are really unordained and must be ranked as laymen. Baptism by such ministers is consequently only lay baptism. If, therefore, so they argue, baptism by lay persons is no baptism, the baptism of dissenters at the hands of dissenting clergy is not valid, and needs to be repeated when such persons become Episcopalians. When this repetition takes place publicly, and especially if the subject of this important rite is a person of note, it finds mention in the press and sometimes opens a public discussion.

This took place during my second year at the seminary, in the case of the Rev. Augustine F. Hewit, now well known as Superior-General of the Paulists. His father was the Rev. Nathaniel Hewit, of Bridgeport, Conn. He himself was licensed to preach as a Congregationalist in 1842, but in the following year he was ordained deacon in the Protestant Episcopal Church. Care, however, was taken to rebaptize him at Trinity Church, New Haven, neither he nor the Rev. Dr. Crosswell believing in lay baptism. This excited much surprise, the baptism being performed publicly in the church. The fact was sharply criticised at the time, especially by Dr. Seabury in the New York *Churchman.* On the contrary, it was defended in the columns of the *Christian Witness.* This repetition of so solemn a rite was occasioned by the fact that in this case neither baptizer nor recipient then believed in the validity of baptism when administered by dissenting clergymen.

All this seems very strange considering that Roman Catholics admit the validity of baptism even by heathens, when the intention is to confer Christian baptism, and the necessary conditions in matter and form are duly observed in the ceremony. Dr. Seabury notices this and quotes the Council of Trent for his authority. There is something very queer in it all, but nothing so very surprising. Episcopalians in this country, and Anglicans in England, are essentially Protestant, and their antics are remarkable when they try to be Catholic.

Enough for the present of professors, and classes, and the framing or setting of seminary life. In our next chapter Tractarianism in America will take on a wider life, with Arthur Carey for its central figure.

CHAPTER III.

ARTHUR CAREY'S CRUCIAL EXAMINATION.—PRACTICAL VALUE
OF THE VIA MEDIA IN A COMPROMISE RELIGION.—LIVELY
FENCING AMONG THE EXAMINERS.—CAREY WARMLY EN-
DORSED AND EXCULPATED.—"NO. 90" SCORES A TRIUMPH.

WHEN at the close of my first seminary year in June, 1843,
the students shook hands with Arthur Carey and with
each other and went home for vacation, few if any knew
that Carey's ordination had been objected to, and that he
was to be put upon trial. When we returned to the seminary
at the close of vacation, both his trial and ordination were
things of the past, but they continued to furnish the most agitating topics of conversation in every part of the United States
where two churchmen could be found.

In no place could it be so much discussed, or contribute so
much to develop the knowledge of doctrine and the appreciation of the real tendencies of Tractarianism as in the seminary
at Chelsea. It furnished thought to every mind that cared to
think, and supplemented well the work done in the classes for
the next nine months. I know of no better place than this to
introduce the history of that trial.

The examination took place June 30, 1843, in the Sunday-
school room of St. John's Chapel, in Varick Street facing
Hudson Street Park, beginning at eight o'clock in the evening.
Bishop Onderdonk presided; and Drs. Berrian, McVickar,
Seabury, Anthon, and Smith, and the Rev. Messrs. Haight,
Higbee, and Price, composed the examining committee. They
had been notified to appear at that time and place (so we find
it recorded in Smith's and Anthon's pamphlet) to try Arthur
Carey and Mr. Blank for Romanizing tendencies.

Mr. Carey was there, but Blank did not appear. Blank
would very gladly have appeared, and there would have been

fine fun during the trial if he had appeared. He would have made the fur fly. Bishop Onderdonk, in fact, put in appearance for Mr. Blank, whose real name was B. B. J. McMaster. "The bishop stated, in relation to one of the candidates, that he would not then be examined, as it had been decided by the faculty that he was to remain in the seminary another year, and that the only duty which would devolve upon the presbyters then and there assembled was the *special* examination of Mr. Carey."

This is all true so far as it goes. There is, however, a very large mental reservation contained in the bishop's statement. It was a convenient reservation under the circumstances. There was an amount of truth attaching to McMaster's absence which it was not prudent to let go to the public. Circumstances have now changed. The trial is now a thing of past history, and moreover the author of these Reminiscences, being no Anglican of any sort of proclivity, and both the trial and acquittal of Arthur Carey, and the subsequent trial and condemnation of Bishop Onderdonk, which was only the natural and necessary sequence of this inquisition held in St. John's Sunday-school, being also things of the past and *des faits accomplis*, I now feel free to give to the public some circumstances of the case which were then suppressed. They have already been briefly referred to in my Reminiscences of Bishop Wadhams. I have there simply stated that McMaster was neither brought to trial nor allowed to be ordained, being too heavy a load for the friendly bishop and other friends of McMaster to carry. I will now add a few words to show why it was so heavy to carry poor Mac through an examination which was sure to be made public.

McMaster, though an earnest man and a most faithful and good Christian, was very unlike Carey in many particulars. His frankness was not like the frankness of Carey. The latter's frankness was due almost entirely to his conscientious truthfulness. McMaster was naturally frank and outspoken. His frankness was of a character which would not only have thrown his accusers into confusion, but would also have made a show of the Right Rev. Bishop and the whole examining committee. It would also have made impossible the exaggerated statements of the examination of Carey put forth by the reverend protestors after the trial and ordination. It would also have made a great difference in the explanatory papers of the reverend doctors who sustained Carey, and which, without denying anything true or affirming anything untrue, yet made a liberal use of the various means of walking around the facts which critics sometimes think they find in the moral theology of St. Alphonsus Liguori.

Dr. Seabury, Dr. McVickar, Dr. Berrian, and the Rev. Messrs. Haight, Higbee, and Price, all put forth either pamphlets, sermons, or newspaper explanations, for the purpose of giving their several versions of Carey's answers to the troublesome questions proposed to him on his examination in order to show what his real belief was; that is to say, whether he was a genuine Episcopalian or a candidate with Romanizing tendencies. The statements of these gentlemen must necessarily be taken for true, *so far as they go.* Their well known characters place them above all suspicion of any wilfully false statement.

Truth, historic truth, however, obliges one, at this late date, who knew Carey well, and from a closer intimacy with him than any of these gentlemen had, to say that not one of these pamphlets contains a full and fair representation of Carey's real sentiments. Moreover, I knew Carey too well to admit that he made a single reply to the many close questions which were so laboriously and painfully pressed upon him which was not true, candid, and open. Any mental reservation which he employed upon his examination, and every cautious distinction of words which he used, was made only to prevent misunderstanding on the part of his examiners, or on the part of the less learned and less disciplined minds of the public. I know him to have been trained to all the niceties of distinction in language which are necessary to constitute a man of true learning; but I know him also to have been "an Israelite, indeed, in whom there was no guile." He had no strong prejudices against the ancient Church Catholic and Roman. He had no bigotry in his heart against Catholics, whom he looked upon as brethren, although by untoward circumstances separated and estranged from himself and from the Anglican communion. But I know that at that time, like McMaster and Wadhams, and many more of us who afterwards became Catholics, he was faithful and true to that communion to which he still clung. His examination was a veritable persecution, although doubtless not so intended by the generality of his accusers.

I wish I could say as much of his examiners. I knew them all, with the exception of the Rev. Mr. Price, of St. Stephen's. If I ever had any intercourse with him, it was slight and has since passed away from my memory. All the others I knew, and my memory retains nothing of any of them unworthy of a Christian man or gentleman. This still leaves me room to say that I consider their published pamphlets to be no full and frank record of Carey's examination, nor of his real sentiments in respect to the Catholic Church.

This obliges me also to say that I have no desire to find fault with these gentlemen for the reserve which they have maintained in their statements to the public of the inquisitorial questions put to Carey and of his replies. They too had behind them, in their congregations or in the general public, inquisitors who were examining them closely and many of them in an unfriendly spirit. They had a right to practise such reserve as every man, however conscientious, may and must, at times, practise.

No man can understand the frank sincerity of Arthur Carey upon his trial who does not rightly understand how the Anglican Church was founded. It was founded by the nervous hand of Queen Elizabeth. She was the Queen of England—she felt herself every inch a queen. She was determined to be the queen of everything in England. She was determined that England's religion should be English, and she believed the best way to make it so was to have an English Church to be ruled in all things by England's government and queen. She must be considered, therefore, as really the founder and really the head of the Anglican Church. She herself and a large body of her subjects were, so far as concerned doctrine, strongly biased in favor of the doctrines of the ancient church. She would gladly have had her church purely Catholic and united in one faith. She would have no pope, however, but herself to cement that union. On the other hand, a large part of her subjects were not Catholic. They not only hated that ancient Roman See which was the *sedes Petri*, but they hated also, for the most part, that old established body of doctrine which constitutes the *fides Petri*. In other words, they were Protestants. They disliked the very name of Catholic, except when carefully explained away.

Nothing but a compromise could bridge over this great difference between her subjects, and she bridged it with such a compromise. All Englishmen who were prominent enough to be reached by persecution were forced by their fears into this compromise. This compromise is to be found in the Book of Common Prayer. In it the catechism is, so far as it goes, Catholic. So is the baptismal service and other special rites. So, mainly, is the entire ordinal of its worship. On the other hand, the Englishmen of Protestant proclivities were propitiated by the "Thirty-nine Articles," which always thunder, or seem to thunder, against Roman Catholic doctrine. To hold these opposing factions in harmony both Articles and Liturgy are so skilfully hammered out that all parties, both Catholics and Protestants, by using the large latitude always practically allowed them, may arrange their consciences comfortably upon the same liturgies and formulas. They were so expected to do in the beginning, and this liberty has at all times been allowed and freely utilized.

"The Reformation of the Anglican Church, as completed and established under Queen Elizabeth," said the *Quarterly Christian Spectator* for October, 1843, "was distinctly designed not to expel or exclude from the ministry of the church such men as Mr. Carey. A strong infusion of sound evangelical or Protestant doctrine was put into the articles and the homilies, and evangelical preaching was tolerated, provided the preacher would closely conform to the canons and the rubrics. On the other hand, the liturgy, and to some extent the homilies, and even the articles, were, we do not say Popish or Romish, but 'Catholic'; and no pains were spared to conciliate and retain in the church every man who was willing to renounce the pope's supremacy, to subscribe the articles, to obey the canons, and to perform the worship of the liturgy as purified and translated. Thus the reformation of the English Church was essentially a compromise, or an attempted compromise, between opposite opinions. It was designed to include, on the one hand the most extreme Protestantism short of that which rejected the hierarchy, the vestments, and the ceremonies, and on the other hand the most extreme Catholicity short of Romanism."

John Henry Newman's famous "Tract No. 90" was professedly written to show how Catholics in the Anglican Church are not bound to interpret and subscribe to the Thirty-nine Articles in a Protestant sense, but may fairly give to its language any literal sense which favors the more ancient and Catholic belief. This Carey also firmly believed, and on this belief all his answers to the questions proposed by his accusers were based. Before, however, we proceed to give the details of that trial it may be well to make a few more words of explanation.

Americans who remember Barnum's museum or his menageries will understand what I mean when I say that the Anglican Church constitutes what Barnum would have called "A Happy Family," in religion. A happy family, according to Barnum's phraseology, was a group of various animals, by nature most hostile to each other, shut up in one cage and obliged *per force* to keep peace. A dog was made to dwell in apparent harmony with a cat, a cat with a mouse and bird. A monkey kept peace with a parrot. The parrot whistled to call the dog, who wagged his tail at the call while he playfully pretended to bite the cat, who showed no signs of fear.

A happy family of discordant elements may be constituted naturally, as, for instance, by the fear of a strong and common enemy. Thus, on the Western prairies may sometimes be seen coming out of the same burrow, or sitting quietly at its mouth, a prairie-dog, a rattlesnake, a little horned owl, and sometimes also a rabbit called by the Western settlers "a cotton tail." For the same reason, so long as the Catholic Church remained powerful in England, Catholic schismatics and Protestant heretics burrowed together, and smoked together the pipe of peace with each other. So soon, however, as the supreme rule of the Roman See ceased to be a power in England, having been crushed

out by blood and sequestration, it became necessary for a royal
Barnum to come in and keep peace among the discordant sects
of Protestantism by the strong hand of power.

The English Church was constituted as a department under
the British Constitution, and no fighting could be allowed in it
except a large latitude of thought and debate, which must not
disturb the established supremacy of the English crown in all
practical matters. Doctrine was, therefore, made to be of little
value in the Anglican Church. Unity in a church so constituted
could never mean a unity in point of faith; apostolicity could
never mean the faith of the Apostles remaining unchanged in
all ages; Catholicity could never mean a common belief in all
nations and in all countries; no standard of holiness could be
maintained which should interfere with appointments to offices
and livings, or the right of communion to any loyal British
subject, whatever he might do, or whatever he might believe.

Out of this compromise, so strange to reason, but which a
long experience has shown to be practically successful, has
grown very naturally a certain principle, or at least motto, among
Anglicans for finding the truth in religious doctrine which is
known by the name of the *via media*. Every Anglican that is
really and thoroughly a typical man in his church is a *via media* man.

For a preacher to confine himself too much to the Thirty-
nine Articles, and to insist upon the most literal acceptation of
their wording, shows an inclination to ultra-Protestantism. To
make too much of the strong flavor of old Catholic doctrines,
which is found in the ritual of the Common Prayer Book, and
especially to evince a pleasure in finding this to conform in so
many respects to the sentiments and worship of Catholics, is
thought by Low-Churchmen to show an inclination towards
Rome, a thing which they hold to be utterly abominable. Yet
in their peculiarly constructed system it is a thing necessarily
to be tolerated. Their church is a religious society in the
civil order. It is a state church, and as such must stand or
fall.

In the Anglican Church the *via media* man best represents,

in point of theology, that keystone of the bridge which keeps the thing together. To all who stand upon the bridge he quotes as a principle of security,

" In medio tutissimus ibis."

To all who look with longing eyes towards either bank he denounces Rome on the one side and ultra-Protestantism on the other. This *cantiloquia*, if I may so call it, of the *via media* preacher, is frequently wearisome to those who look for positive doctrine. I have known it to become even ludicrous. I have already said that during my seminary course I acted as superintendent of the Sunday-school of the Church of the Nativity, on the east side of the city. It was considered a good idea to gather the Sunday-school children to the morning service, placing them in front between the congregation and the chancel. They were very troublesome to manage in this exposed position, but it was thought to be a pretty thing to do, reminding both them and their parents of our Lord's love for little children. I occupied the front pew just behind them. My duty it was to keep them quiet. At morning service one Sunday a French-Canadian officiated ; it was something strange for the little children to hear a gowned preacher speaking in so peculiar an accent, and it made my task that morning unusually difficult. But when they heard him pronounce, with his strange accent, the familiar words : "My dear bretteren, Rome is on tis side, and ultra-Protestantism is on tat side ; you must keep in te meedle, between te two," the irreverent youngsters could no longer maintain the least restraint. They disturbed the good minister most seriously, and made a great show of me. I was responsible for their behavior. In point of fact the *via media*, as a way of arriving at any positive truth in the religious or moral order, is always absurd, if not ridiculous.

In order truly to understand the positions of the various actors in this examination of Arthur Carey, and to interpret their utterances fairly, it is necessary, I think, to view the whole affair from this stand-point. Carey was sincerely Catholic, and believed that under the original compromise he had a right to

be, and that, without any necessity of attacking the Roman
Catholic Church or any of its members, he could honestly remain where he was and advocate Catholic principles. Drs.
Smith and Anthon were square Protestants, and in all positive
Catholicity of doctrine or worship they saw the horns and the
hoofs. The rest of the board of examiners, with certain differences in point of latitude, were substantially *via media* men, but
strongly inclined to so much of Catholicism as the Anglican
bridge would hold. The Right Rev. Bishop was very much in
the same position, with this additional responsibility, that he
had to keep the "boys" of the diocese in order, and not let
them break things or disturb the diocese.

In the evening of June 30, 1843, as already stated, the examiners of Arthur Carey assembled in the Sunday-school room
of St. John's Chapel, and his formal examination began. It was
on Friday, less than two full days previous to the Sunday morning appointed by the bishop for the ordination of candidates to
the diaconate. It was well understood by all parties present at
this trial that Drs. Smith and Anthon appeared not only as
judges but as accusers. Carey was, in fact, a member for the
time being of Dr. Smith's congregation. He was a regular attendant at St. Peter's, and a teacher in the Sunday-school. To
Dr. Smith and his vestry he applied for the required certificate
recommending him to the bishop for orders. This certificate
Dr. Smith, after a close examination, had refused to sign.
Carey then obtained a certificate from Trinity Church. Trinity
if I remember right, was the cathedral, or pro cathedral of the
diocese, and a sort of mother of churches for the whole State
of New York.

Drs. Smith and Anthon opened the trial. They proposed to
put to the candidate certain questions which they had prepared
in writing, and the answers to which they wished to have written down by Carey. This was objected to by some of the
judges. They seemed to consider it a threat of future publication in case that Carey should pass safely through his trial and
be ordained. The bishop decided that these written questions
might be put in any order the prosecutors desired, and that
notes of Carey's answers might be taken and read to him; but

that Carey should not be required to formulate his answers in writing.

The first question proposed by Dr. Anthon was the following:

"Supposing entrance into the ministry of the Protestant Episcopal Church in this country were not open to you, would you or would you not have recourse, in such case, to the ministry of the Church of Rome?"

Objection was made to this question by some of the committee. Dr. Seabury said it was a hypothetical question and a trap for the conscience, and advised Carey not to answer it. Dr. McVickar remarked that they might as well ask Mr. Carey whether, if he had lived in the time of the patriarchs, he would have married two wives! Carey, however, expressed his willingness to answer, and he did so. He said that the case supposed would be a painful one; that he did not know what he should do; that certainly he should come to no hasty decision on so grave a matter; that he should spend two or three years at least in deliberating on the subject; that at the expiration of that time he possibly might seek admission to the ministry in the Church of Rome; but that he thought it more probable he should remain a layman in his own church, since he was satisfied with it, was attached to it, and had no disposition to leave it. The two interrogating doctors, however, insisted on a categorical answer, or the nearest to it that might be. Mr. Carey then replied:

"Possibly I might, after due deliberation, but think that I should more likely remain a layman in our own communion, as I have no special leaning towards theirs at present."

I can add some little testimony of my own in regard to this point from my remembrances of Carey. A few days before this examination, when Carey was in my room, I expressed myself with some considerable feeling in regard to a seminarian who was thought to have strong inclinations to become a Roman Catholic. Carey looked up to me with an air of surprise and said:

"Do you think it would be so very wrong to join the Roman Catholic Church?"

I replied I thought it would be very wrong for one who knew so much as the student in question. Carey remained very thoughtful, but pursued the subject no further. There can be little doubt that he would have found it difficult to make the leap at that time ; but I never knew him to speak unfavorably of the Catholic Church, or of any Catholic doctrine, or of any Catholic as such.

Before the examination proceeded beyond this point the bishop decided that any member of the committee might offer to Carey such advice, or make such interruptions to questions, as would insure a full and fair trial.

The second question proposed by Dr. Smith was as follows:

" Do you hold to and receive the decrees of the Council of Trent ? "

Answer: "I do not deny them—I would not positively affirm them."

To satisfy inquiries of the committee Carey explained :

1st, That he did not regard the Council of Trent as œcumenical, and of course that he held its peculiar definitions to be open points, and not of faith; 2d, That in what he might say favorably of the decrees of Trent, he took the decrees in the mere letter, and not as interpreted by the Romish system, and the concurrent sense of Roman divines; and, 3d, That he held the Roman Church responsible for the errors of her system, and the teaching of her doctrines.

These explanations, omitted in the account given by Drs. Smith and Anthon, are given on the authority of Dr. Seabury and others who favored Carey. Their substantial correctness cannot well be doubted ; but I knew Carey too well to believe that he used the word Romish. I never knew him to apply an insulting word to the Church Catholic and Roman, or to Roman Catholics.

Proceeding then with the examination, a third question was proposed :

" Do you, or do you not, deem the differences between the Protestant Episcopal Church and the Church of Rome to be such as embrace *points of faith ?* "

Mr. Carey's reply was at some length, and was not taken

Old
East
Building
(Restored)

Rev. Samuel Seabury.

down *in ipsissimis verbis* by any one. Drs. Smith and Anthon report that they understood the answer to be, that—

"If these differences be understood to be matters of doctrine, they would embrace points of faith; but if, as is believed, they are matters of opinion, they would not."

Dr. Seabury says that such a report of Carey's answer seems to him mere jargon, and that a young man so well instructed could not have made it, and did not. Dr. Seabury's own account seems equally jargon to Catholics. Dr. Seabury reports that Carey explained that by the word faith he meant the fundamental or essential faith, which, says the doctor, is common to the two churches of England and Rome, the differences between the two communions pertaining to the superstructure, and not to the foundation. To a true Catholic theologian the idea of a truly Christian Church building up such a superstructure of unreliable faith upon a foundation of essential faith is a jargon quite as ridiculous as that imputed by Drs. Smith and Anthon to Carey. It is absurd to represent the Church Catholic and Roman as holding the same essential faith with the Church Anglican and un-Catholic.

Carey is also represented as having stated that the differences between the two churches were more than matters of opinion; that they were grave doctrines, the truth of which he was not prepared either to deny or positively to affirm. These words are simple and intelligible. Many converts from Anglicanism to the true church have formerly stood in the same painful position of doubt. Carey's heart was honest, but his soul was still in the dark.

The next question brought up was one of these grave points of doctrine on which Sister Rome disagrees with Brother John:

"Do you, or do you not, believe the doctrine of Transubstantiation to be repugnant to Scripture, subversive of the nature of a sacrament, and giving occasion to superstition? If you do not, how can you *ex animo* subscribe the 28th Article of our Standards?"

Carey's answer, when condensed and reduced to writing, was as follows:

"I would answer, in general language, that I do not hold *that* doctrine of transubstantiation which I suppose our Article condemns; but that, at the same time, I conceive myself at liberty to confess ignorance on the mode of the Presence."

I have a remembrance of Carey's examination upon this point derived, I think, from one of the editorials published at the time in the *Churchman.* When Carey was pressed to state whether he believed that the substance of the bread and wine still remained after consecration, he replied that he found a difficulty in affirming this to be his belief since there was a doubt of the existence of any substance in bread and wine apart from its appearances, even before the consecration. In support of this he referred to the Philosophy of the Anglican Bishop Berkeley. This is said to have caused much confusion in the minds of Carey's examiners, and no little merriment outside.

In answer to the next question, Carey said that he considered the denial to the laity of the cup at communion as a severe act of discipline, but he declined, however, to say that it was an unwarrantable change in a sacrament.

Carey was then asked :

"On which church do you believe the sin of schism rests in consequence of the English Reformation—the Church of England and, by consequence, the Protestant Episcopal Church of this country, or upon the Church of Rome?"

Under advisement of Dr. Seabury he at first declined to answer the question as being an historical one. The bishop decided the question must be answered. The reply then given was, that in some respects schism rests on both sides. He considered both churches in communion with the Church of Christ.

Dr. Anthon then read the seventh question on the list :

"Is the Romish doctrine of Purgatory in any respect maintained by our Standards?"

The bishop asked Dr. Anthon what view *he* entertained on the doctrine of Purgatory as held by the Church of Rome; to which Dr. Anthon replied that, "with due respect to the chair, *he* was not under examination." Carey, to whom the distinctions in " Tract No. 90 " were very familiar, answered that he considered the Standards as condemning the doctrine popularly held to be the Roman doctrine.

Carey's answer to the next question was based on the same distinction.

" Is there any countenance given in the doctrinal Standards of our church for the idea that the departed can be benefited by the prayers of the faithful, or by the administration of the Holy Communion? And is not *that* idea condemned by Article 31 of our church?"

Carey's answer, as agreed to by both friends and accusers present at the trial, was substantially as follows: "that he supposed that idea was not condemned in that article; his opinion being that the language of the article was popular language, pointed at a popular opinion which was held against the Church of Rome."

Dr. Seabury, commenting afterwards on this question, is not a little merry at the expense of Drs. Smith and Anthon. The two doctors either forgot for the moment, or were not willing to admit with many theologians of their church, that " the Eucharist is a sacrifice of prayer as well as a sacrament of Communion."

" How they or any other creature, human or inhuman, on the earth or under the earth," wrote Seabury, "could ever have dreamed of the departed being ' benefited by the administration of the Holy Communion ' passes all comprehension."

In answer to the ninth question Carey said :

" I do not, either to myself or any one else, attempt to prove a doctrine out of the Apocrypha." " The Holy Spirit may have spoken by the Apocrypha, and the Homily asserts the same thing."

The bishop here drew out, by several questions skilfully put to the accused, certain quotations from the Homilies, supporting Carey's view. Carey finally said:

" I would not fault the Church of Rome for reading the *Apocrypha* for proof of doctrine."

Dr. Smith next asked :

" Can there be a doubt that, in separating from the Church

of Rome, the Church of England embraced more pure and Scriptural views of doctrine? And is not the Protestant Episcopal Church in this country at present more pure in doctrine than the Church of Rome?"

Answer: "There can be a doubt, on the ground that the Church of England *retained* doctrinal errors, viz., the doctrines of Puritanism, . . ."

Mr. Carey said that the Roman Breviary and Canon of the Mass were preferable to the Liturgies and Communion Service of the Church of England. The Breviary contained more copious citations from Scripture, and a richer variety of services. The Roman Canon was in closer conformity with the ancient liturgies. The Communion Service was deficient in not having the Oblation and Invocation. For the purposes of congregational worship, Carey was of the opinion that the Anglican Liturgy was better as being in a tongue understood by the people.

Carey's answer to the eleventh question, "What construction do you put upon the promise of conformity to the doctrines, discipline, and worship of the Protestant Episcopal Church?" is very ludicrously reported in the pamphlet put forth by the two prosecuting doctors. They represent him as saying that "he did not consider the articles as binding our consciences in points of faith." Of course Carey said precisely the contrary. It was precisely those declarations in the Articles that were matters of positive faith, which required belief and bound his conscience. He considered that there were matters contained in the Articles which did not present points of faith, and only required an exterior conformity. He quoted in support of this position many divines of his own church, especially the famous Anglican theologian Bishop Bull, who says, speaking of the Thirty-nine Articles, that the church "only propounds them as a body of safe and pious principles, for the preservation of peace, to be subscribed and not openly contradicted by her sons."

Carey also submitted to the committee that American Episcopalians are not required by any canon to give, as in England, a distinct and *ex animo* assent to the Thirty-nine Articles, but only a general promise of "conformity to the doctrines and worship of the Protestant Episcopal Church," for which he quoted Bishop White as his authority. Carey, however, waived this personal right, and said that he was willing to give his *ex animo* assent to the Thirty-nine Articles as the assent is given in the English Church. By this he undoubtedly did not mean to give up his right to interpret the articles in the sense given by "Tract No. 90."

It is impossible for me to give the twelfth question on the list of Drs. Smith and Anthon, either virtually or substantially. The examining committee seem to have fallen into a sort of confusion ; a variety of questions were put by different examiners and objected to. Some were allowed and some not. It is probable that whatever No. 12 really was, it stands covered by other questions afterwards substituted.

Amongst the answers thus elicited I may state the following : Carey said that as to the invocation of saints, "he did not fault the Church of Rome, provided the invocation was confined to the '*ora pro nobis*,' or intercessory form." It is not probable that Carey intended himself to be understood that he would have nothing to say to a departed saint except when he wanted something. He simply meant to express his belief that there was nothing they could do for us, except through their interest before the Throne of Grace. The Pope could say as much.

When asked whether he considered the Church of Rome *now* to be in error in matters of faith he replied :

"It is a difficult question, which I do not know how to answer."

At the conclusion of the examination Arthur Carey was requested to withdraw. The presbyters present were then called upon by the bishop severally to express their opinions. Drs. McVickar and Berrian, and Messrs. Haight, Higbee, and Price, expressed themselves as quite satisfied with the fitness of Carey for orders. Dr. Seabury added that he "should esteem it a privilege to present the candidate for orders, as he had sustained his ordeal most nobly." Drs. Smith and Anthon's sentiments were as decidedly unfavorable to the candidate and to the conduct of the examination. The latter declared that "in the whole course of his ministry he had never attended an examination conducted in a manner so painful, and in which so many *impediments* were thrown in the way of his arriving at a definite knowledge of the candidate's views."

The bishop was not prepared to give his decision at that time, but said, with emphatic dignity, that when his determination should be formed he would carry it out without regard to consequences. His decision was afterwards speedily made in Carey's favor. The next Sunday saw him ordained. This was the practical application of "Tract No. 90," and a momentary triumph for Tractarianism.

The next chapter also will be entirely devoted to Reminiscences of Arthur Carey.

CHAPTER IV.

PROTEST AGAINST ARTHUR CAREY'S ORDINATION.—CENTRAL
POINT OF A GREAT STORM.—CAREY'S FAMILY.—FURTHER
DETAILS OF HIS LIFE.—ASSISTANT TO SEABURY.—EARLY
DEATH AND BURIAL AT SEA.—NEWMAN'S INTEREST IN
CAREY.

THE ordination of Arthur Carey took place at St. Stephen's
Church, New York City, on Sunday morning, July 2,
1843. Bishop Onderdonk ordained him, assisted by Dr. Ives,
Bishop of North Carolina, and also Dr. Berrian and two
others of the examining committee. I was present at this ordination. In my Reminiscences of the Life of Bishop Wadhams I have given a pretty full account of all that was extraordinary in the proceedings, relying simply upon my own
recollections. I propose now to give a history of the same affair drawn chiefly from an account furnished to the New York
Churchman of July 8, 1843. The writer signed himself N. E. O.
—Neo-Eboracensis Onderdonk (?)—and is supposed to have
been Bishop Onderdonk himself.

During the ceremony of that eventful Sunday, the usual call
having been made upon the people to show cause, if any existed, why the candidate, or any of the candidates, should not
be ordained, the Rev. Hugh Smith of St. Peter's and the Rev.
Dr. Anthon of St. Mark's, habited in their canonicals, arose
successively from a pew in the middle aisle and read their several protests against the ordination of Arthur Carey. My father
and I occupied a pew in the body of the church just under the
front of the organ-gallery. The whole scene was in full view
before us, and I have forgotten very little of what helped to
make it memorable. I have taken care, however, as already
stated, to fortify my own recollections by accounts of spectators, published at the time, especially that of the bishop himself.

Each protest, says N. E. O., had been drawn up with much lawyer-like formality, and contained the accusation that the candidate held doctrines adverse to those of his church, and too nearly bordering on popery, and referring for proof to statements and circumstances within the bishop's knowledge.

The manner of the reverend gentlemen was slow and distinct, and, it seemed to me, as solemn as utterance could make it. When the two doctors had finished their protest, "the bishop rose," says N. E. O., "and expressed himself to the following effect, and, I believe, in the following words:

"'The accusation now brought against one of the persons presented to be ordained deacons has recently been fully investigated by me with the knowledge and in the presence of his accusers, and with the advantage of the valuable aid and counsel of six of the worthiest, wisest, and most learned of the presbyters of this diocese, including the three who are assisting in the present solemnities. The result was that there was no just ground for rejecting the candidate's application for holy orders. There is consequently no reason for any change in the solemn service of the day, and therefore all these persons, being found meet to be ordained, are commended to the prayers of the congregation.'"

My own memory of the event brings nothing to my mind to correct this statement of the bishop's words as given in the New York *Churchman*, with one exception. My recollection is very distinct that the bishop's concluding words were: "And, therefore, I shall proceed to ordain *all* these candidates, notwithstanding the scandalous interruption of these Reverend Protesters."

The bishop then recommended them to the prayers of the congregation, and Bishop Ives began the reading of the litany. The service went on without any further interruption. It is stated without contradiction, so far as I know, that the two protesting clergymen took up their hats and walked down the middle aisle to the front door during the litany. The rest of the congregation remained.

The impressions on my own mind when witnessing that morning's service still remain unchanged. Believing himself to

REAR VIEW WEST BUILDING OLD EPISCOPALIAN SEMINARY, CHELSEA SQUARE, NEW YORK.

be doing his duty by ordaining Carey, the bishop could not have gone through with his part with more admirable tact and dignity. For the same reason, if Drs. Smith and Anthon were right in opposing Carey's ordination by a public protest, they were right also in not remaining to witness it.

"Mr. Arthur Carey has suddenly, and at a very early age, become a historical personage," said the *Quarterly Christian Spectator* of October, 1843, in reviewing these occurrences. This is true enough ; and strange it is that one so gentle and peaceful as Carey should suddenly become the cause and centre of a bitter strife which shook the entire world of Anglicanism in the United States. The bishop and his advising and consulting presbyters were suddenly put upon their defence. A matter adjudicated and disposed of by the authorities of the diocese had somehow got itself appealed to the whole body of Episcopalians in the country. The bishop and all his counsellors who had taken part in Carey's ordination were obliged to account for themselves to the public, or the whole case would go by default. Disapprobation of what they had done was beginning to be uttered *semper, ubique, ab omnibus ;* and unless they could do something to turn the tide of opinion they were likely to be overwhelmed. We give them credit, continues the *Christian Spectator*, for the boldness, skill, and manfulness with which they have conducted their defence.

Each and every one of the examining committee was obliged by the public excitement to account for himself by some published statement, explanatory of his action and his reasons for it. Bishop Onderdonk was the first, appearing, as we have seen, in a communication to the *Churchman* signed N. E. O. This was followed by various editorials of Seabury in the same periodical, selections from which were afterwards collected into a pamphlet. Drs. McVickar and Berrian soon followed with their versions and explanations. Opposed to these and in vindication of themselves then appeared Drs. Smith and Anthon with their pamphlet. Messrs. Haight, Higbee, and Price were also forced to appear in the public arena. Not one of the committee was able to remain silent. Not only the public excitement, but a special turmoil in their several congregations, forced them into some explanation which helped to add new fuel to the gathering fire. From the pamphlets put forth by these reverend gentlemen, and from the comments of religious and other periodicals, and the columns of the daily press, the history of the Carey examination, and of its more immediate and far-reaching results, can be gleaned.

One result of this agitation was the establishment of a new periodical, which took the name of the *Protestant Churchman.* Its object was to counteract the influence of Dr. Seabury's *Churchman.* Its projector and first editor, the Rev. R. C. Shimeall, initiated a series of sermons or lectures against Tractarianism, for the delivery of which he enlisted such prominent preachers as the Rev. Drs. Tyng, Anthon, Smith, Bedell, Balch, Stone, etc.

I do not propose to follow up this great wave of excitement, discussion, assertion, contradiction, calls to arms, appeals for peace, which filled for so long a time all our Anglican presses, pulpits, and social hearths throughout the land. Some things of this kind will come in later on. Our present business is with Arthur Carey. Poor, secluded, unobtrusive victim of circumstances, he was thus suddenly called out from a sort of hermitage to which his soul had grown accustomed, to be a centre of wonder and study. This is no place to leave him. It was the will of God to take him away quickly from the storm which he had so unwittingly excited—a watery grave lay just before and near him—and yet he was too great a part of that great storm to be suddenly dropped from these Reminiscences.

I now propose to give to the reader an account of all I can gather or recall of his whole life not already given.

Arthur Carey was descended from that ancient Devonshire family of Carys which derives its surname from the Manor of Cary in that county. In Domesday book the name is spelt Kari. Arthur's father, John Carey, removed with his family to the United States in 1830. John Carey's father, grandfather, and great-grandfather, all bore, like himself, the name of John, and were born in London. This first John Carey, born in 1687, was the oldest son of Francis Carey, who was born at Lisgar, Ireland, and died in Yorkshire. His father was Patrick Carey, who was born in Ireland in 1622, but died at Teignmouth, De-

vonshire, in 1634. Patrick was the fourth son of Sir Henry
Carey, the first Viscount Falkland. The various branches of
this family scattered through England and Ireland are traceable
to their common source not only by their origin in Devonshire,
but by their coat of arms won by Sir Robert Cary, of Cocking-
ton. The chronicle, as quoted by Burke in his *Landed Gentry*,
runs as follows :

" In the beginning of the reign of Henry V. a certain knight-
errand of Arragon having passed through divers countries, and
performed many feats of arms to his high commendation, arrived here in England, where he challenged any man of his
rank and quality to make tryal of his valor and skill in arms.
This challenge Sir Robert Cary accepted ; between whom a
cruel encounter and a long and doubtful combat was waged in
Smithfield, London. But at length this noble champion van-
quished the presumptuous Arragonois ; for which King Henry
V. restored unto him good part of his father's lands, which, for
his loyalty to King Richard II., he had been deprived of by
King Henry IV., and authorized him to bear the arms of the
Knight of Arragon, viz., ' In a field silver, on a bend sa. three
white roses,' which the noble posterity of this gentleman continue to wear unto this day ; for according to the laws of her-
aldry, whosoever fairly in the field conquers his adversary may
justify the bearing of his arms."

Sir Edward Cary, of Marldon, in Devonshire, who succeeded
to his title in 1616, was one of the leading Catholics in Devon,
and suffered unrelenting persecution on account of his faith.

Descendants of his known as the Carys of Follaton, County
Devon, are Catholic and connected by marriage with the noble
Catholic families of Stafford, Petre, Clifford, Dillon, Kenmare, etc.

Other Carys of the same Devonshire stock are as strongly
bound to error as Protestant alliance can make them, being
descended from Mary Boleyne, the aunt of Queen Elizabeth,
the foundress of the Protestant Church of England. Mary's
son, Henry Cary, was created Baron Hunsdon by his royal
cousin.

Arthur Carey, the most noble subject of these Reminiscences,
was born, all untitled and all unlanded, in England, in the vi-

cinity of London, June 26, 1822, and removed with his father to the United States in 1830. He had two brothers, John and Henry. John Carey has a son still living, Mr. Arthur Astor Carey, of Boston. Our Arthur Carey, of the Chelsea Seminary, spent the first years of his life at home in New York City, with the exception of two or three years during which he was under the care of Bishop Hopkins, of Vermont. There at the age of twelve a desire was kindled in his heart to devote himself to the ministry. This purpose, which his father approved, never afterwards left him. I remember that he always spoke with esteem and affection of Bishop Hopkins, although the development of Carey's mind during his seminary course led to a wide divergence from this early friend in matters of religious doctrine and opinion.

In January, 1836, he entered the sophomore class at Columbia College. He graduated there in 1839, receiving the highest honors of his class, and delivering the customary Greek oration on that occasion. The only rival to contest this honor with him was a son of Dr. Henry Anthon, of St. Mark's Church, then located in Eighth Street. It is a singular coincidence, though otherwise a fact of no special significance, that this rector of St. Mark's should be one of Carey's examiners, his chief accuser, and afterwards, conscientiously enough no doubt, protesting solemnly against his ordination.

It was said amongst the students at Chelsea Seminary that upon his graduation at Columbia College this remarkable boy—for in years Carey was nothing else—was offered a professorship if he would remain. No honors, however, could stir a soul like his, and he entered the General Seminary of his church at Chelsea. His age when he entered upon his theological course there was only seventeen years and four months. This course he completed in June, 1842. The esteem created in the minds of the faculty at Chelsea by his extraordinary talents and early wisdom, as well as by the moral beauty of his character, was the same as that which remained behind him when he left Columbia College.

I have no hesitation in applying to this extraordinary young man the words so often quoted in Catholic hagiology to designate those choice souls among ourselves who die in early youth leaving behind the odor of a holy life : " *Consummatus in brevi explevit tempora multa.*" During that single year at the seminary when Carey was my nearest neighbor, which brought us together daily, he certainly aimed at Christian perfection in his life. I had conversations with him on that subject. In these I took occasion to explain to him the views of certain perfectionists, so-called, amongst the Presbyterians ; and in particular those of Dr. Phinney, a president and, if I remember right, the founder of Oberlin College, Ohio.

At the time when I first knew Phinney he was a revival preacher among the Presbyterians, very earnest and powerful in his eloquence, argumentative in his methods of persuasion, and quite destitute of all affectation and flourish. Carey had also reflected much on the question of Christian perfection, but his views were very different from those of Dr. Phinney. Perfection, in Carey's mind, was not any acquirable state of sinlessness, but a constant progress on the way towards a high mark, with a changeless resolution to discard all sin even the least, and embracing in desire all the Christian virtues. On his recommendation I purchased a work on Christian Perfection, by Law, the non-juror. This book I read very carefully and enjoyed very much. If Law had better understood, or at least better heeded, the distinctions which Catholics make between commandments of God which bind our consciences under penalty of sin and punishment, and counsels of God which, mindful of our weakness, only invite us to higher ways of perfection, his doctrine would be quite Catholic.

Many a sincerely pious Protestant takes pleasure in singing that beautiful song whose constant refrain is

> " Nearer, my God, to Thee,
>   Nearer to Thee."

Many such an one drinks in much of the wonderful sweetness attaching to the words, and yet is far behind either Carey, or Law, or even Phinney, in the appreciation of true Christian perfection. The reason is that, unlike these three, they have not learned to discard the immoral doctrine of justification by faith alone, without need of holy works or advance in virtue.

In Carey's case, be it understood, Christian perfection was something far beyond an appreciated doctrine. His life was holy and lovely. For one year, during which our chamber doors faced each other, I saw him constantly and closely, but for all that sight or sound could tell, to me his character was faultless. He was not within the visible fold of the church, but certainly many graces that streamed forth from that church had reached him and produced their fruit within him.

He was at this time, as I have said, very young, younger than myself. Not only I, but every one in the seminary, including the most venerable among the professors, looked up to him with respect as a man of God. How short a time to gather so much virtue! It could not be difficult for such a young man as that to secure permission from the faculty of the seminary to keep his room there for yet another year after his graduation when he would arrive at the canonical age for ordination. This enabled him to use the library of the institution while he pursued his studies in private.

During this time, apparently so quiet for him, that great storm was brewing which broke upon his solitary habits and gentle heart like a thunderbolt. It was then, as we have seen, that occurred the public charges against his fitness for ordination. It was at the close of the seminary course in June, 1843, that his trial on these charges before Bishop Onderdonk and a committee of clergymen chosen for that purpose was held. A few days after, on July 2, Bishop Onderdonk, overruling these charges, ordained him at St. Stephen's Church; and thus closed his career as a seminarian, though not quite all his seminary associations. Several of his old companions, not only those studying at the seminary but others still remaining in the city, took pleasure in visiting him at his new lodgings. This was down-town, at 101 Charlton Street. McMaster, in particular, passed many an hour with him. They walked together, talked together, and read together, eagerly discussing every new publication that issued from Oxford, and prospecting together over

every storm that threatened their church and every opening in
the clouds that gave hope of coming sunshine.

Carey was now in orders, with a career before him, a life to
lead in the ministry, and high duties to perform. The reader
will be anxious to know where he was stationed, what charge
was assigned to him, what position he assumed. In short, it is
necessary to give some account of his after life in the face of
that world in which he had become so prominent a character.

But Carey needed rest. He had been in a state of excitement. This excitement
before and after his or-
dination had been so great
upon one of his nervous
and feeble constitution
and sedentary habits that
his exhausted nature de-
manded repose. He had
neither strength nor heart
to enter upon any labori-
ous work in the ministry.
It was, however, no matter
of conscience with him,
and he allowed himself,
as usual in such cases, to
be overruled by the urging
of Bishop Onderdonk and
the advice of friends. He
accepted for six months,
at least, an invitation from
the Annunciation Church
—then on the corner of Prince and Thompson Streets—under
the charge of his friend and patron, Dr. Seabury. He was to
assist the doctor as deacon, with a salary of five hundred dollars.

JAMES A. McMASTER.

It is easy to conceive that many eager friends, to say nothing of many others in a curious public, would resort to this
church on Sundays to see him and hear him preach. Of
Carey's parochial labors I have little remembrance of my own.
I had duties on Sunday in a different direction. I was superin-

tendent of a Sunday school in a far different part of the city, near the East River, and my route to it lay in another direction. Once, however, in the autumn of 1843, I made an occasion to go and hear him preach. I went in company with McMaster, and well I remember the day. The crooked streets which served as our roadway there would have made the walk to me a perfect labyrinth, but I had no difficulty to get there with such a guide. McMaster must have been a regular attendant on Carey's preaching during the short time it lasted. He knew every twist and turn that lay before us. Bleecker Street, which we followed for awhile, serpentine as it is, seems to me now a good type of our own crooked course towards Rome. We were not very long in getting to our destination that Sunday morning, for McMaster's long strides and rapid movements hurried me forward till my breath was nearly gone. I seem to see him now, with coat sleeves that never reached his wrists, and trousers that never covered his ankles. I think he was a little proud of this peculiarity. Carey himself, who was McMaster's chief or at least nearest model in all things possible to imitate, was rather negligent in his dress. At least his pantaloons always bulged out at the knees; I think, however, caused chiefly by frequent kneeling. I do not remember the subject of Carey's sermon that morning, but I carry with me still a vivid picture of him as preacher. To me Carey himself was a sermon, that needed no words. He stands in my memory like a young St. John, Evangelist; or one like Newman, Dalgairns, or the Paulist Father, Francis Baker, my own dear friend and long companion on the missions.

Carey did much more than preach in the Annunciation parish. His duties were not necessarily very burdensome. Yet to a man like him, so earnest and so conscientious, to accept any responsible position is to begin active work. In Carey's case souls were at stake, and a life of leisure was not to be thought of. In a letter to his friend and fellow seminarian, Edgar P. Wadhams, dated October 23, 1843, Carey gives some account of how his time was occupied while serving as assistant to Dr. Seabury.

"I preach on Sunday afternoons," he writes, "and open the

church for Wednesday and Friday services, morning and evening, and saints' day services. I was afraid to begin with daily
services, and the doctor thought better not at present. He
says I may do anything I please, and he will never interfere
with me, but always support me, which is pleasant, at all
events."

Dr. Seabury, in a funeral sermon preached in the following
April on receiving the news of Carey's death and burial at sea,
enlarges somewhat upon Carey's account of himself, or rather
tells us what Carey's humility would never allow him to say or
even think.

"You saw"—he said from the pulpit, looking down upon
many tearful eyes that met his own—"you saw the sober and
serious earnestness with which he threw himself into his parochial duties. You saw his faithfulness in the Sunday-school, his
solicitude for the poor and afflicted, and his love for all
the members of Christ. You were impressed with the natural-
ness and quiet solemnity with which on week-days and holy-
days, as well as Sundays, he performed the services of the
church. You heard his sermons on every Lord's Day during
the short time he was with you, and you know the depth, the
simplicity, and the unction with which he preached to you the
Gospel of Christ. But after all it was not any one thing, so
much as the manifest godliness of this young man, the fire of
holiness pervading all that he said and did, and communicating
itself to all who heard him, which gave him the hold which he
had on your hearts."

Not only the fire of holiness which Dr. Seabury attributes
to Carey, but also a wondrous facility for fortifying his arguments in preaching or in conversation by apt and telling words
of Scripture, is easily accounted for by the following fact. We
learn on the same authority that it was Carey's rule to read
through the Old Testament three times and the New Testament five times a year. He believes also that he gave three
hours daily to private devotional exercises, unless unavoidably
interrupted.

The funeral sermon of Dr. Seabury, from which I have
gathered the above information and much that follows, is hap-

pily preserved in the New York State Library, amongst its bound documents.

Carey commenced his services at the Annunciation Church on the second Sunday of October, 1843, about three months after his trial and ordination. "He continued to discharge them until the 29th of December, on which day he took to his bed of a fever. After two or three weeks the fever abated, and hopes were entertained of his recovery. But the energies of his system did not rally; and he was left in a declining state which, in the judgment of his medical advisers, rendered expedient a voyage to Cuba. For four or five years before he had been affected with incipient disease of the heart, which, though not very urgent, showed itself in occasional paroxysms, when different exciting causes called it into action. On Sunday, March 17, he was enabled to ride to church and to join in the prayers of his loved people for his safe and prosperous voyage. After this grateful but most agitating service he conversed for a few minutes with some of his anxious and still lingering flock, and at the doors of the church laid his attenuated hand upon the heads of some of the Sunday-school children, for whom he cherished a most lively and affectionate concern.

"On the 23d of March he embarked with his father for Havana. The voyage, though not stormy, was rough and disagreeable; but every discomfort was borne by the sufferer with the same meek and placid resignation by which his life had been distinguished; not a murmur escaped his lips on any occasion of annoyance. On the 1st of April he raised a very small quantity of blood, but not enough to excite any alarm. On the 4th of April, however, he had a return of the same symptom, and continued to bleed from the lungs, though very slowly, for about an hour, when without any apparent diminution of strength, and with his eyes open and calmly fixed on his father, without a struggle or even the slightest perceptible movement of muscle, he expired at the early age of twenty-one years and ten months. . . ."

"On the next day (Good Friday) the body was committed to the deep, in the full belief that the earth and the sea will simultaneously give up their dead. The church burial service

was impressively read by Mr. Grosvenor, a gentleman connected
with the Seaman's Friend Society, the subdued and reverent
demeanor and tearful eyes of the passengers and crew evincing
the hold which the gentleman-like manners, and the mild and
meek deportment of the deceased, had gained on their hearts.
The burial took place about fifteen or twenty miles north east
of the Moro Castle, on the very day on which the deceased,
had he lived, would have landed in Havana."

Not alone Captain Joseph Spinney, but all on board the
vessel, showed the most generous consideration at this trying
time.

I cannot refrain from transcribing here a touching reminis-
cence of Carey recorded by Rev. A. F. Hewit, in his memoir
of Baker : "For a long time afterward his poor father might
be seen every day standing on the Battery and gazing wistfully
out to sea, with mournful thoughts, longing after the son whom
he had lost."

It may seem to some of my readers that I have yielded too
much to imagination and affection in portraying the character
of Arthur Carey, and overdrawn the picture. Or, it may be
thought that I have rested too much upon the testimony of
other friends, prejudiced like myself in his favor. For this reason I now turn willingly to a witness who must be acknowledged on all hands to be free from any such bias. Dr. Hugh
Smith, rector of St. Peter's, may be set down as in many respects Carey's most forward and unrelenting adversary. Carey
was a Tractarian ; Smith was bitterly opposed to Tractarianism,
and must rather be classed even as a low-churchman, if not an
evangelical. Dr. Smith was Carey's principal accuser, both before the trustees of the seminary and when put upon examination before his bishop. He was the principal and earliest mo-
tor in opposing Carey's ordination, more forward and urgent in
opposition than Dr. Anthon, the other accuser. He believed
Carey to be alienated from the doctrine and discipline of the
Anglican Church, and more consonant in mind and heart with
what he called Romanism. For these reasons he considered
him unfit for orders, and protested solemnly against the action
of Bishop Onderdonk at St. Stephen's Church, during the very

ceremony of ordination and while that church was crowded with spectators. For the same reasons he continued to denounce Carey's bishop after the ordination was over in pamphlets, sermons, and contributions to the newspapers. Is such a man to be looked upon as biased in Carey's favor? On the contrary, must we not take him as a most disinterested and honest witness in every word which he utters in Carey's praise? Will it be said that perhaps Dr. Smith did not know Carey well enough to testify to the moral side of his character? He ought to know him and know him well. During the four years that Carey roomed at the seminary he was a member of the doctor's congregation; he was a teacher in the doctor's Sunday-school; he attended service regularly at the doctor's church, and received communion at his hands. It was to Dr. Smith, as pastor, that Carey felt himself obliged to apply for a canonical certificate recommending him for ordination, meeting, of course, with a refusal. No higher testimony to Carey's moral character can be brought than that of such a man. Then let him come upon the stand. This is what he says:

"I had, from an early period of his connection with St. Peter's, understood that he (Carey) embraced the doctrines of the Oxford school; but such was my conviction of the purity and excellence of his Christian character, and of his quiet and studious habits, and of his love for truth, that I was not only willing, but anxious, to have the benefit of his services in my Sunday-school."—*True Issue for the True Churchman.*

To this need be added only one more tribute. It is that of a periodical as unfriendly to Carey's doctrinal tendencies as Dr. Smith himself. The *Quarterly Christian Spectator* of October, 1843, reviewing Carey's ordination, commented in these terms upon his character:

"He appears to have been not only diligent and successful in study, but eminently amiable and blameless in his deportment, the pride of his teachers and the joy of his friends."

From this time forward an "angel face" will no longer be found in these reminiscences. I am not aware of any biography or even sketch of Arthur Carey which is not sadly fragmentary, or which pretends to completeness of any sort.

About sixteen months after Carey's death, in the latter part of August, 1845, when James A. McMaster, Isaac Hecker, with myself, all fresh converts to the Catholic Church, were passing through London on our way to the Redemptorist novitiate at St. Trond, in Belgium, the first named separated from us long enough to visit John Henry Newman, then still connected with the Anglican Church, and dwelling in retirement at Littlemore, near Oxford. When introduced into his library McMaster found him occupied in a manner not altogether strange to so busy a student. His right foot rested upon the seat of a chair; he stood bending over a book which he held in his left hand, the contents of which he devoured simultaneously with a sandwich administered to his mouth by the right. When McMaster informed him that he had become a Catholic and was about to become a religious, Newman expressed no surprise and made no unfavorable comment. Only two months later he was himself a convert. McMaster spoke to him of Carey, who was not unknown to him. The doctor showed much interest in Carey and asked many questions concerning his career. When, however, McMaster urged him to write a biography of him, as one of his own most prominent and gifted disciples, the doctor declined. Carey, he said, was an American, and only some American more closely and intimately connected with his life could do him justice.

All those who could have filled such a *rôle* have either passed away or are little likely to undertake the task. For want of a better biographer, and that the memories which I can supply may not be lost at my death, I have made this too brief account as complete as my scant means allow me. His family motto was: "*Deo cari nihilo carent*"—"The dear to God are beyond want." I venture to add these words, *Requiescat in pace.*

CHAPTER V.

THE opening of my second year at the seminary found me
in many respects unchanged from what I had been twelve
months before. In regard to the diversities of faith and opinion
which existed among Episcopalians it would have been hard to
classify me. I could no longer be called an Evangelical. The
scales had fallen from my eyes. Luther was no longer a hero.
The reading of D'Aubigné's history had left him mirrored to my
mind as an ambitious, restless, and dogged man, but one whose
loud professions of zeal were merely the shams of a demagogue,
while his private life showed grovelling instincts inconsistent with
a man inspired by a divine influence. And so it was in some
degree with all the other reformers I knew of. Whatever good
there might be in them, they shone no longer like stars in my sky,
and with me they carried no authority. Nevertheless I was still
Protestant, and in my eyes the Reformation continued to wear a
certain providential character. It had proved, I thought, a good
broom. The same hands that wielded the broom had also
moved away much useless furniture.

Some of the Tractarians in England loved to call themselves
"Apostolicals," and there was a good deal about their movement which seemed to be apostolical. William George Ward,
one of the leaders of this stamp in England, in his *Ideal of a
Christian Church*, proposes as a practical test to show whether a
church is apostolical or not, to load the existing framework
with all possible good. "If it will bear it, all is well. If not,
God himself has solved for us the question and the system
breaks down of itself."

I had long felt a strong calling to missionary work. If the

Anglican Church lent itself zealously and generously to missionary labors, it afforded at once a strong test of her genuineness
and opened to me a field in which I could joyfully labor. The
General Seminary had its missionary society. I had joined it
at the beginning of my course, and I commenced this, my second year, with a new interest in its meetings. I was elected
president of this society. Its members took much pleasure in
reading such accounts as they could procure concerning church
missions in foreign parts, and we discussed them at our meetings.

At one of these meetings we were favored with the attendance of a church missionary from China. He entertained us
with an account of that country and of the wide field there
opened to missionary enterprise. He had little, however, to say
of any actual converts made, or of any very tangible influence
exerted upon the inhabitants. He had brought home with him,
at the expense of the Church Missionary Society, a Chinese who
was, he told us, a man of note in his own country, a scientist
and of remarkable intelligence. This yellow gentleman, he acknowledged, was no Christian and gave no evidence of any tendency in that direction. He made some disturbance during the
missionary's address by his restlessness. Our meeting was in the
seminary chapel. The organ there excited the curiosity of the
Chinaman, and, without any apparent sense of discourtesy, he
left his seat among the auditors to examine the organ, looking
over and sounding the keys with great care, and kneeling down
behind the box to scrutinize the pipes and the complicated
action. Under these circumstances the lecture could not last
long. We were all collected very soon about him, much amused
by his movements. He laughed with great delight, and made
various signs to show how well he understood the character of
the instrument and how its work was done.

In point of fact this Chinese philosopher on exhibition at
our meeting had nothing whatever to do with missionary labor
in China. Any Chinese curiosity in a show-box would have answered the same purpose. When the missionary wanted audiences he helped to draw. It paid him also to lend his services
in this way, yellow skin, slanted eyes, and pig tail, to the Church

Missionary Society. It was not a little disappointing to many earnest minds in our society, that this sight of a Chinaman was about all that our memories could retain of the lecture on missionary experience in China.

The Church Missionary Society, however, scores a better point against other Protestants, or thinks so, when a live bishop of any kind whatever appears from the East. It was about this time that Mar Yohannan, a Nestorian bishop from the mountains of Ooroomiah, was introduced to the notice of American Protestants. He came over to this country under the auspices of the American Board of Missions, and was received with great acclamation by pious Presbyterians everywhere. He was no convert to anything, but he hobnobbed very comfortably with his new friends and made a good thing of it. I saw him at Saratoga. He spent some days at our house, on my father's invitation, and was a great curiosity. My mother was quite delighted to receive him as a guest. It seemed to her a blessing to have him. His friendly connection with foreign missionaries was in her mind an all-sufficient guarantee. Everything about him seemed right to her, except that he was an inveterate smoker. She abominated smoking as something irreligious at least, if not wicked. He was quite satisfied, however, to pass the greater part of his time on the front piazza, where he could smoke freely. His Nestorianism did not seem to need repairing, but his clothing did, and the girls of the family set themselves to work to make him a new outfit. I remember well the great glee with which they surveyed the immense amount of blue cloth necessary to sew up into trousers.

A theory was started that Mar Yohannan and his people were descended from the lost tribes of Israel, and this was a great boom for the American Board. These, it must be remembered, were the days of Charlotte Elizabeth—" Old Crazy Bess," as McMaster was pleased to call her in his irreverent style. She was then still living. Her writings were in wide circulation, and Protestant piety had been excited to the highest pitch of interest in all that regarded Israelites, and everything that looked forward to the conversion of the Jews. Episcopalian Protestants also, at least those of the high-church school, were much inter-

ested in Mar Yohannan for peculiar reasons of their own. He
was a bishop, and, although schismatical in worship and hereti-
cal in faith, had an undoubted succession from the Apostles.
Several of their bishops sought out interviews with him and endeavored to draw from him some expressions recognizing a
fraternity of this kind. So far as I remember their efforts were
unsuccessful. Mar Yohannan knew very well on which side his
bread was buttered, and either evaded their questions or put
them to confusion by replies more consonant with the Evangelical tone of the Presbyterian missionaries with whom he con-
sorted.

The greater part of the students at the seminary were not
merely Episcopalians in name, but strongly attached to that
feature of church government which divides their organization
into dioceses with a bishop at the head of each diocese, with
presbyters and deacons under these as distinct orders of the
clergy. The majority of them, indeed, believed this feature
of their church to be not only a thing of divine institution,
but necessary to constitute a true Christian ministry. They
believed in the necessity of an apostolic succession. To constitute
this succession it is necessary that a bishop's official right to represent Christ should be traceable back to the Apostles, through an
uninterrupted series of ordinations. This taken alone, without an
historical union of belief and a visible brotherhood in obedience to
one rule, is, to, be sure, a very slender thread. It separates them
very little from the confused crowd of Protestants with whom in
doctrine they agree so closely. It assimilates them very slightly to
the ancient church from which they differ so widely. On the other
hand, their difference from all Oriental schismatics is as wide as
ever. There is no community of faith between them, and yet Episcopalians are well known to be proud of a certain supposed unity
with these ancient Eastern churches.

What I have said is enough to account for the general
interest taken by Episcopalians in Dr. Southgate, who became a
very prominent figure in the religious world at the very time when
Tractarianism was at its height. He was sent to Constantinople
as an Episcopalian missionary in 1840. He was called home
and sent back again in 1844, with the valuable title of bishop

attached to his name. It was hoped by this means to establish an alliance, or at least to manifest some sort of unity, between the Protestant Episcopal Church and the Greek churches of the Eastern world.

We students of the seminary became much interested in Dr. Southgate, and particularly those of us who belonged to the missionary society at Chelsea. It seemed to present high hopes to all those of us especially who looked forward to a missionary life as one that might become our own. Dr. Southgate was made ready to appear at Constantinople with all the prestige attaching to the rank of bishop. We, too, might soon follow, and under the shadow of his apostolic powers gather in Greeks, Armenians, Nestorians, to—well, it is hard to say what! These Oriental churches had a real antiquity, and an acknowledged episcopate, which we had not. If they took us into partnership it would set us up. In return for this brotherly embrace we could communicate to them that superior spirituality which we had derived from Protestantism.

All this seems to me, of course, very foolish, very dreamy and very unpractical now. In our seminary, however, at that time, it did not seem so. There was plenty of matter in this mission to Constantinople to excite young hearts to a high enthusiasm. I do not remember that Carey, McMaster, or Everett, or any advanced Tractarians, took much stock in it.

I may as well at once say here by way of anticipation that Bishop Southgate's mission to Constantinople proved to be a great failure. He was not recognized by Eastern Christians as a bishop, or as differing essentially from other Protestant missionaries. He only succeeded in raising a war of recrimination between himself and Presbyterian or Congregational missionaries who had preceded him in that field. And this war was fought over again before the American public. I will give the history of it. It helped to hurry forward some anxious hearts on their way to Rome.

It has already been said that Bishop Southgate began his missionary labors at Constantinople in 1840, at which time he was a priest. From October, 1844, he continued his services there as bishop. In 1850 he resigned his charge and returned to America. We know of no mission since to replace it. No mention is made of any in the *Church Almanac and Year Book for 1892.* It will throw light upon the hopes and disappointments of many hearts, both in the seminary and outside of it, to give some little detail of the position of Dr. Southgate at Constantinople, and of the circumstances that made his mission fruitless. Much of its history can be found in printed pamphlets of the time. One of these is entitled *A Vindication of the Rev. Horatio Southgate.* This pamphlet, issued for the information of members of the bishop's own denomination in the United States, contains not only a vindication of his conduct against charges made by the American Board of Foreign Missions, but also counter-charges against the Presbyterian missionaries in that city. In answer to this was published a " Reply " reviewing the whole history of the quarrel.

According to the bishop's statements the Congregationalist missionaries at Constantinople had so far concealed their real character that an impression generally prevailed among the Armenians that they were clergymen of the English Church and were for some time supposed to be bishops. This impression was strengthened by their assuming the Episcopalian clerical dress, using the Common Prayer Book, making the sign of the cross in Baptism, and other like practices unknown to Congregationalists at home.

These charges are not denied by the missionaries.in their " Reply " as facts, but they repudiate the motive given, that they wished to pass themselves off for Anglican ministers. They allege as a counter-charge that a great change had taken place in Dr. Southgate's demeanor towards them upon his returning to Constantinople as a bishop. Upon his first coming to Constantinople he was very cordial and friendly. He sat down at the communion table with them, received the sacrament from their hands, and took part with them also in the administration of it. He attended public service regularly with them on the Sabbath, sometimes preaching for them and sometimes listening to their preaching ; and often had he bent the head together with them in prayer, he taking his turn without book or stated form.

After his visit to America, from which he returned to Constantinople as bishop, he was entirely metamorphosed, and determined to act on the most exclusive high-church principles. As a man he professed to be ready to live with them on terms of civility; but as a Christian, and especially as a Christian minister, he seemed to wish to have no visible relations with them. He would not consent even to have a prayer-meeting in common which they formally proposed, lest it should be supposed by others that he recognized them as true ministers of Christ, equally with himself.

The hopes founded by Episcopalians upon Dr. Southgate's appearance in Constantinople, and the apparent motives for his changed demeanor towards the missionaries of the American Board, may be seen in great part in the fact that he brought a letter, signed by seven bishops of his church, addressed to the Greek and Syrian patriarchs, in which the proposition is formally made for a certain kind of friendly alliance and co-operation.

Another point of missionary policy is to be noted here. On the one hand, it seemed all-important to Bishop Southgate's mission to Constantinople to make him appear as much as possible like an Oriental bishop. On the other hand, it would never do to have him mistaken by the Orientals for a Roman Catholic bishop. It was for this reason that the Rev. A. F. Hewit, now a Catholic priest and Superior of the Paulists, was not allowed to go with him, as he desired. Hewit was known at that time to have strong inclinations in favor of Roman Catholic doctrine. He was already very much of a Tractarian and of a character too frank to hide it. Appleton's *Cyclopædia of American Biography* puts this in still stronger language. It says of Hewit : " He was selected to accompany Bishop Southgate as a missionary to Constantinople, but the missionary committee refused to ratify the appointment on the ground that Mr. Hewit held beliefs that were distinctively Roman Catholic."

The committee were wise in their generation. Hewit was too earnest a Christian to play the part of a *via media* man very satisfactorily, or impose himself upon Orientals for anything but what he really was. In 1846 he was received into the Roman Catholic Church, and is well known in that Church for a long, strongly marked, and most successful missionary career.

Failures of missionary enterprises like this of Southgate do not suddenly and completely extinguish the hopes that lie in faithful and ardent hearts or destroy their confidence in the organizations to which they belong. What matters Constantinople or all the ancient Eastern churches on a map of the world? So Anglicans sometimes say both in England and in America. Have we not a great missionary history to show in Hindustan and in the rest of our Indian empire? In order to counteract any dangerous inferences that might be drawn from his praise of the " Early Jesuit Missions in North America,' Bishop Kip says of them : " There is not a recorded instance of their permanency, or their spreading each generation wider and deeper, like our own missions in India." This bold statement is in singular contradiction to actual facts.

In 1869 Sir William Hunter was entrusted by the Indian government with the statistical survey of India. According to his report the census of India for 1891 opens to us the following statistics : The total number of Christians in all India, including Burmah, is 2,601,355. Of this number about 700,000 are Protestants of one or other denomination, rather more than 300,000 are Jacobites, who hold the doctrines of the Eastern Church, and 1,594.901 are Catholics. Of these latter 221,000 are Syrian Catholics, in communion with Rome but having their own rite and clergy, and the rest are Catholics of the Roman rite.

How bold, bald, and untruthful is Dr. Kip's boast in face of these documentary facts! Even India herself, that country so thoroughly and terribly subjugated to British rule, that golden mine of British wealth, that fairy field of Anglican labor, has harvested far less to the English Church than to the influences of the Catholic religion, all poor and unsupported as it is. Sir William Hunter says that "the Roman Catholics work in India with slender pecuniary resources." He also allows that "the priests of the Propaganda deny themselves the comforts considered necessaries for Europeans in India. They live the frugal and abstemious life of the native, and their influence

reaches deep into the life of the communities among whom
they dwell."

These facts were not so well known to the seminarians of
my day at Chelsea ; not even to those of the missionary society,
who were best informed in these matters. There prevailed
amongst us, however, much suspicion of the actual truth, and
much gloomy foreboding in regard to the future.

In comparing Anglican missionaries with the early Jesuit
missionaries of North America Dr. Kip says:

"Our own church has equally her *Acta Sanctorum.* . . .
The annals of no church give a loftier picture of self-sacrifice
than that furnished by Henry Martyn, when he abandoned the
honors of academic life and exchanged his happy home at
Cambridge for the solitary bungalow at Dinapore—the daily
disputes with his Moonshee and Pundit—or the bitter opposition of the Mohammedans at Shiraz. And nowhere do we
read of a nobler martyrdom than his, when he lay expiring at
Tocat, without a friend to close his eyes or a sympathizing
voice to address him. So, too, it was when Heber left the
peaceful retreat of Hodnet, to suffer and die under the burning
heats of India."

Far be it from me to decry the merits of Martyn or of
Heber, or of other pious ministers in the Anglican fold or any
other. It is, nevertheless, neither true nor edifying to put these
estimable men on the same platform with Isaac Jogues, René
Goupil, Brébœuf, Lalemant, Rasle, Daniel, Junipero, Abella,
and a host of others who literally left all their natural friends
to dwell in perpetual danger amongst savages, ending their lives
in torturing, starvation, or violent death. A room called the
chamber of martyrs in the college of the *Missions Étrangères* at
Paris is full of mangled remains, of instruments of torture, and
other tragic mementoes of missionaries of the same heroic
mould, who in our day have ended their lives in China.

Neither Martyn nor Heber can be set down as martyrs.
Whether either can fairly be considered as a confessor for his
faith is very questionable. That they were both very estimable
and pious Christian men is to be admitted freely.

Henry Martyn was a real missionary, and constantly during

his whole career in India and before that, while dwelling in England, and waiting as a candidate to be ordered to his field of labor, showed signs of a true zeal for the conversion of the heathen. The best evidence of this zeal is the fact that, refusing to take up his abode in Calcutta or any other large town, already crowded with Europeans and with clergymen ministering to Europeans, he clung firmly to his station at Dinapore, where he was in the very midst of a heathen world. There, also, although made safe against danger by the presence of British soldiers, he was deprived of nearly all such social life as could naturally be agreeable to him. There was much of privation and voluntary sacrifice in this. There was much also of missionary work, the most congenial and agreeable of which was his literary labor in translating the Bible and Common Prayer Book into Hindustanee and Persian. How nearly such a life approaches to the heroic must depend upon that degree of courage and endurance which one attaches to the idea of heroism. What seems to detract most from the heroism of such a career as Martyn's is a weakness of love-making, in which we find him engaged while in England, kept up until the very time of his departure,—and the fact that some years after, while at Dinapore, he writes home to this old love, whose name we only know as L——, offering her his hand in marriage. This offer was declined. The marriage of a man involves many duties, and these not a little engrossing. Duties not only to the wife who has received his vows, but to a family of children, which will in the course of nature form about him. To a missionary devoted to his work as a divine and special vocation, this married life, however attractive, is incongruous. It must necessarily interfere with the engrossing demands of apostolic labor. It is difficult to harmonize it with a life of missionary heroism.

Martyn would probably have done much better where simple heathenism only existed, unsupported by any learned philosophy. He himself was little provided with liberal learning. Quite deficient in anything like systematic theology or philosophy, he was unable to cope with the trained minds he encountered even at Dinapore. His task was still more difficult at

Shiraz. There he came in contact with Mohammedans, Brahmins, Buddhists, Jews, and others, many of them well trained to philosophic distinctions. It seems strange that once when closely questioned by Mohammedan teachers in regard to the person of Christ, he should have endeavored to explain the Christian doctrine of the Incarnation by saying that *we did not consider his human nature eternal* (see Sargent's *Memoir of Martyn*, chap ix. p. 320). This was very satisfactory to the Mohammedans, as well it might be.

Mrs. Heber, widow of the bishop, in her biography of her husband, gives us his estimate of Henry Martyn as follows:

" Many of Martyn's sufferings and privations he saw were caused by a peculiar temperament, and by a zeal which, disregarding all personal danger and sacrifice, led that devoted servant of God to follow, at whatever risk, those objects which would have been more effectually attained, and at a less costly sacrifice, had they been pursued with caution and patience."

I give this estimate for what it is worth. I have not been criticising the wisdom or patience of Martyn, but his title to rank as a hero among missionaries. Whatever his title in this roll of honor may be, he cannot be classed as a typical Anglican, or as in any way an example of piety or virtue deriving its source from the Church of England. Although holding orders in that church, he was in all his religious views and in the spirit and tone of his piety an Evangelical Puritan. This shows itself in a certain disagreeable technical dialect found everywhere throughout his diaries, journals, and letters, which belongs to Puritan piety, and is in no way characteristic of Anglicanism. This is not at all astonishing, since the books which he most delighted in for pious reading were, after the Bible, the works of Baxter and John Newton, while his chief model as a missionary was David Brainerd.

Bishop Heber cannot rightly be classed with Henry Martyn. It is difficult to look at the bishop as being a missionary at all. However gifted with other qualities which entitle him to respect, his vocation to heathen lands came when the British cabinet gave him the appointment of Lord Bishop of Calcutta. His appointment found him officiating tranquilly as rector at

Hodnet. He sailed for India with his wife and child in 1823, and remained in occupation of his diocese until his death in 1826. This death was caused by imprudently taking a cold bath after a day of labor and exhaustion. He visited his vast diocese faithfully, as every faithful bishop must, confirming and otherwise ministering not only to Europeans, but to native converts, when such fell in his way. There was no special privation or self-sacrifice in this. The whole crowd of Englishmen who flock to Hindustan meet the same inconveniences and dangers. To be Lord Bishop of Calcutta was to rank high in India, second in importance only to the governor-general himself. When setting out to visit his vast new diocese, in the second year of his residence in India, as he himself tells us, he started on his journey up the Ganges with three vessels, two besides the one in which he and his domestic chaplain, Rev. Martin Stowe, travelled.

"One of these," he writes, "is a cooking-boat, the other for our luggage and servants; · . . . twelve servants are thought a very moderate travelling establishment for myself and a single friend; and that the number of boatmen for the three vessels amounts, I believe, to thirty-two."

On leaving his boats to travel by land at Allahabad his train or caravan consisted of "twenty-four camels, eight carts drawn by bullocks, twenty-four horse servants, including those of the archdeacon and Mr. Lushington, ten ponies, forty bearers and coolies of different descriptions, twelve tent-pitchers, and a guard of twenty sepoys under a native officer." All, servants and sepoys, were heavily armed. At every settlement where he arrived he was met by British officials, and was received with distinction by rajahs, princes, and native kings.

This is all very right. We only mention it to show that Bishop Heber's vocation in India was not one of a nature to rank him among the heroic missionaries of history.

Bishop Heber undoubtedly ranks high among Christian poets. He could not have united the spirit of a Christian with the lofty conceptions of a poet without being able to appreciate the highest type of a Christian missionary. One is not surprised, therefore, to find amongst his poems this beautiful tribute. I give only one stanza of one of his best hymns:

> "The Son of God goes forth to war,
>   A kingly crown to gain;
> His blood-red banner streams afar!
>   Who follows in his train?
> Who best can drink his cup of woe,
>   Triumphant over pain,
> Who patient bears his cross below,
>   He follows in his train."

That Dr. Kip should have instanced Bishop Heber as a specimen of this class of heroes must be attributed to the fact that he is the author of that celebrated hymn, the opening words of which are familiar throughout the world—

> "From Greenland's icy mountains,
>   From India's coral strand,—"

I do not give any more because all the beautiful lines that follow are known by heart to so many thousands. A poet's special vocation, however, and his inmost character, are not necessarily indicated by a single hymn however widely spread. Bishop Heber is also author of the following beautiful lines addressed to his wife, who remained at Calcutta while he was visiting his diocese:

> "If thou wert by my side, my love,
>   How fast would evening fail
> In green Benagla's palmy grove
>   Listening the nightingale!

> "If thou, my love, wert by my side,
>   My babies at my knee,
> How gaily would our pinnace glide
>   O'er Gunga's mimic sea."

There are seven more stanzas in the same strain, all beautiful poetry and all coming undoubtedly from his innermost heart.

The reader may perhaps wonder that in these reminiscences of a seminary life I should linger so long upon details concerning missionaries not connected with our institute at Chelsea. I have done it for a special purpose. In the first place, I have wished to show that Episcopalians are not behind other Protestant Christians in their appreciation of missionary work. In the second place, this work in their church puts on some special features of its own. These features are suitable to its own peculiar pretensions. It claims an ancient and apostolic character. It claims also a certain sort of Catholicity, something which binds it to all ancient churches throughout the world. These two claims are founded upon their supposed apostolic succession. All this, as I hope, will serve to show how amongst candidates for orders inclined to Tractarianism, but earnestly anxious to save their confidence in their own church, there grew up a yearning after a life of missionary monasticism. This last point will find its development hereafter. This yearning led to hope. This hope led to a break-up. Patience, good reader. Land ahead!

CHAPTER VI.

FURTHER MISSIONARY ASPIRATIONS.—"CRAZY RICHMOND."—
TYNG'S LECTURE.—WARD'S "IDEAL OF A CHRISTIAN CHURCH."
—MEDITATION.— PRIVATE RETREATS. —PARISH MISSIONS.

THE reader of this series of reminiscences will already have
seen that the missionary question opened a large field of
hope, doubt, and anxiety to myself and to other Anglican
students within the seminary and outside. The attraction
to such work was especially strong in minds progressing
towards Catholic faith. During my second year's course at the
seminary I made acquaintance with a very peculiar sort of person, an Episcopalian minister of the diocese of Rhode Island,
whom I frequently met at a house near the seminary where I
boarded. It was the Rev. James C. Richmond. He was distinguished by the sobriquet of "Crazy Richmond" from his
brother, who was, if I remember right, an officiating clergyman
at Manhattanville. This James Richmond had a sort of roving
commission in Rhode Island, and loved to carry the title of
missionary. On learning that I was president of the missionary
society at the seminary and much interested in missionary enterprises of every kind, he urged me to join with him in doing
something with the neglected poor in New York City. On
Sundays, when going to a Sunday-school attached to Nativity
Church, near the East River, I frequently passed through
Tompkins Square, where a large number of poor people loved
to gather on all Sundays and holidays of leisure to find fresh
air and amusement. Richmond had heard me speak of this.
To his quick intelligence and eager activity it suggested an
opportunity to labor among the poor. He would conduct the
services of the church and preach in the open square, while my
part would be to lead in the singing. I would very willingly
have engaged in an enterprise of this kind if I had felt more

confidence in Mr. Richmond's prudence, and had not feared that our movements might come to clash with the authority of Bishop Onderdonk. Upon this he offered to apply to the bishop for permission, although he did not seem to think it necessary.

This application and its result is incidentally recorded in a pamphlet published in 1845, during a *mêlée* of pamphleteers who rushed into print after the memorable trial of Bishop Onderdonk. This pamphlet is entitled *Richmond's Reply to " Richmond in Ruins."* In this publication Mr. Richmond had occasion to refer to two visits made by him to Bishop Onderdonk, and says:

" He [the bishop] has also mingled my call upon him July 4 with another call in August or September, which I made after a conference with Clarence Walworth in reference to my duty of preaching in the German language to the churchless and almost Godless Germans that assemble around Tompkins Square. On the last visit I said not a word that could be tortured into an implication of a shade of a wish to 'return to his diocese.' On the contrary, after saying that I was desirous of preaching to the Germans, and felt that I was bound to do so by my ordination vow, 'to seek for Christ's sheep that are scattered in this naughty world,' and that it was not through duty, as I previously told C. W., but for courtesy that I waited on him, having already not only a privilege but an obligation thus to officiate, with the consent of the nearest rector or rectors; he asked, on my reference to the *Catholic Oak*, what was there accomplished. 'My friend, if you are doing so much good in Rhode Island, why not remain there?' I replied: 'I intend to do so; but having one spare Sunday, I thought it would be best to help you and begin here; then the people who wish to talk can spend as much of the winter as they like in discussing the merits of the movement, and the question of my sanity, pro and con, and by next summer they will be tired of the talk, and when I come again it will be an old story, and the ice will have been effectually broken, and the way prepared for others.' He wittily replied, 'I am afraid, my friend, it would freeze over again this winter.' I waited a moment, weighing and appreciating the *bon mot*, and then replied nearly thus, in my stupid way: 'Bishop, the ice is of long standing; the neglect of the poor is old and crusty, and do you not think by breaking it up once now, the new ice would break more easily next summer?'"

My recollections accord very well with those of Mr. Richmond above given, except in two or three particulars. The Germans in the vicinity of Tompkins Square were not at this time destitute of church privileges. There was a Catholic Church near by the square, on Third Street, with preaching in German. Those who frequented the square were by no means all Germans. To many English was their native tongue, and I think that nearly all the crowd could speak it, and were embraced in our intentions. I think, also, it was not intended to confine ourselves to one Sunday. This, of course, could do but little good. The bishop refusing permission, of course our project failed.

It is not really necessary to the purpose of these reminiscences to say anything more here of Mr. Richmond. Nevertheless, having been once introduced, it may not be too much of a digression to add one passage more from this same pamphlet. It develops still more the peculiar character of the man. It shows somewhat his idea of himself and his consciousness of the light in which he stood in the eyes of many others. It shows also the light by which he surveyed his critics and estimated the value of their opinions:

"My 'erratic peculiarities' I gratefully admit, and thank my stars that I am not so *humdrum* as most other people, who walk with pious care in their forefathers' steps, just as some farmers always plant their potatoes in the old way because it was good enough for their grandfathers."

I have never since this occasion, so far as I remember, been called upon to take part in any religious services conducted in the open air, except at the laying of some corner-stone or monument; or when in some parish, at the beginning of a mission, it was thought necessary to speak to a crowd in the street and invite them to services in the church; or when at its close a memorial cross was erected in the open air; or

when soldiers on their way to war were gathered in camp to
hear Mass, make their Communion, and listen to preaching. I
have dwelt, perhaps, a little too much on this Tompkins
Square project, and on the figure of this peculiar man. I have,
however, an excuse for it. It will be necessary for him to
appear again in the course of these reminiscences in matters of
deep import to the Chelsea Seminary, to the New York diocese,
and to Anglicanism generally.

The agitation which pervaded the air at the time of my
seminary course, and which was at its highest height at that
time, was fed from many sources, and reached to every
Anglican circle. It was fed by every new tract which issued
from Oxford; by the *British Critic,* which was the principal
organ of the Tractarian movement; by the Lives of the Early
English Saints, and by other volumes of books and published
sermons for and against the movement; by every attempt to
engraft some Catholic practice into Anglican worship; and by
every attempt on the part of authority, either civil or ecclesiastical, to stifle the movement. All these things reached the
seminary and became subjects of eager discussion. It was a
contest between old sleep and new life. It could not be kept
out of any society instituted at the seminary. I recall to mind
an instance where our society for the encouragement of foreign
missions divided itself into high and low church partisans, the
question being whether a certain sermon or lecture delivered in
the Church of the Ascension, before the society, should be
published by it or not. The lecturer had been the Rev. Dr.
Tyng, a prominent clergyman of that day. A motion had been
made and carried at one of the regular meetings of the society,
that the reverend doctor should be asked to furnish the manuscript of his lecture for publication. Some of the members who
had been absent were dissatisfied with this, and a new meeting
was called to reconsider the matter. A few words will suffice
to explain the cause of dissatisfaction, and of the contest which
ensued.

Dr. Tyng was a very prominent and talented low-churchman.
This alone would not have been enough to constitute a difficulty in publishing his lecture. It happened, however, that

there was a vacancy at this time in the bishopric of Penn-
sylvania, and Dr. Tyng was known to be a candidate for the
office. His lecture had been quite free from anything that
savored distinctly of evangelical low-churchmanship. Considering the peculiar atmosphere which prevailed at the seminary
this was not to be wondered at, but a thing which excited

much remark was that the
reverend doctor had assumed a certain high-church
tone in some parts of his
lecture. This was looked
upon by many as an insin-
cere bid for support in his
pretensions to the mitre,
and the majority of our students, who were either Tractarians or at least high-
churchmen, were not will-
ing that the seminary should
seem to lend any endorse-
ment to the man.

At the second and special
meeting of the missionary
society, called as above stated, the attendance was unusually large. A motion
was offered, if I remember
right by Dr. Everett, to re-
scind the action of the regular meeting. An eager
contest ensued. The low-
churchmen were in the mi-

REV. WILLIAM EVERETT.

nority, but, led by Harwood, they showed a great skill in endeavor-
ing to protract the debate, which was very animated, and to prevent any decisive vote being taken before adjournment The high-
churchmen were equally determined, equally skilful, and equally
watchful. I have reason to remember this contest very well.
I was president of the society at the time, and it was my first

experience in ruling troublesome points of order in a sharp contest. It seemed to me as if all the discordant elements that are combined in Anglicanism had broken their compromise and had gathered into that one room where our meeting was held, while it had become my duty to bring the confusion back to order. The Rev. Dr. Everett, however, now rector of the Church of the Nativity on Second Avenue, was the spirit which really presided at the meeting. He managed the forces of the majority, pressed his motion to a decisive vote, and so the matter ended. The lecture was not printed.

A few of the members of this society not only felt strongly interested in foreign missions, but actually looked forward to a missionary life for themselves. This interest, however, had not been originated by anything going on in the Anglican Church, nor did it find there any serious encouragement. I do not know of any seminarians of my time that ever entered into the missionary field. All the life that existed in Episcopalianism was concentrated in a struggle to keep itself alive. All really earnest hearts anxious to be engaged in gathering abandoned or neglected souls into Christ's fold were driven about wearily from hope to hope, not willing to sink back into despair, and yet not knowing where to settle. Surely, they argued, that great church to which we belong must somewhere have a heart corresponding to the pulsations which we feel.

It was such a time as this and such a juncture of circumstances that saw the appearance of Ward's *Ideal of a Christian Church*.

The book itself did not appear until the close of my second year at the seminary, namely, in June, 1844, but much of the substance of the volume had been published during that year in the *British Critic*, of which both Ward and Dr. Newman had been editors.

The numbers of the *British Critic* had always been eagerly welcomed by Tractarian students at the seminary, until the violent opposition excited by it in England brought it to a sudden stop.

We did not all of us find time or means amidst our studies to read these numbers of the *British Critic*, but McMaster,

Everett, and a few others of the higher classes did. I have already given in my Reminiscences of Bishop Wadhams a letter of Arthur Carey's, written from his lodgings in Charlton Street, a few lines of which I will repeat here. Carey says to his friend in the Adirondacks:

"McMaster is now sitting by my side: he has just come down from the seminary, and is now reading to me out of the October number of the *British Critic.*"

In my mind's eye I seem to see him now, with those large young eyes beaming with intelligent interest at Ward's disclosures in regard to Catholic meditation and Catholic mission work, with a smile on his lips at McMaster's more emphatic ebullitions of delight.

It is well known that Ward's *Ideal* not only led to its author's public condemnation by the authorities at Oxford, but was the culmination point at which Tractarianism broke down, and after which a crowd of converts, both in England and America, came fluttering into the ark. This makes it necessary for me

CARDINAL NEWMAN.

to revive the memory of this book and give some idea of its contents.

The principal significance of Ward's *Ideal*, and that which made it so intolerable to its adversaries, was that it was so pointedly practical. It represented the Roman Catholic Church as full of practical piety, and, on the other hand, represented the English Church as lost in a lifeless formality. For brevity's sake I shall confine myself to such parts of this remarkable work as touch upon the care due from the Christian Church to her candidates for orders; how such a church must train them to piety, virtue, and Christian perfection, and how she needs must hold them to their daily duties as ministers of religious worship, instruct and animate them in the work of saving souls, and particularly the souls of those who are the most destitute and abandoned.

With abundant quotations from recognized works, this aspect of the Roman Catholic Church is exhibited by Ward, and the absence of similar provisions in the English Church is pointed out: Meditation, to make the truths of religion more vivid; constant examination of conscience, that sin may not be passed over or forgotten; occasional retreats, as a fresh start after neglect; the literature of ascetic theology and hagiology to stimulate in the service of God by example and precept; the confessional for pardon and direction; moral theology to save priests from caprice, and give them the benefit in advising their penitents of the experience of the Corporate Church,—here, says Ward, are the spiritual weapons of the Church of Rome; and where, he asks, can we find their counterpart in England?— (*William George Ward and the Oxford Movement*, by Wilfred Ward, pp. 279 and 289.)

Mr. Ward does not content himself with general declarations in favor of such practical work among Roman Catholics. He gives an account of the actual Rule of Life carried out in a French Ecclesiastical Seminary, as furnished him by the rector. Such a rule of life will be nothing new to Catholic readers. They may find it interesting, however, as showing how plainly this fearless Anglican divine shook the red scarf before the eyes of John Bull. John, of course, received it as a bitter taunt, but not a few of John's children were pained to the heart by it, and grieved over it as those grieve who gaze upon graces forfeited.

The French rector divides this rule of life adopted in his seminary into eighteen points of practice. For brevity's sake I will content myself with merely naming the most of these points. These are: vocal prayer at half-past five in the morning, followed by meditation ; after this the holy sacrifice of the Mass; visiting the altar where the Holy Eucharist is kept, and praying before it for a quarter of an hour each day ; a spiritual reading each day from some book of piety ; reciting the chaplet—that is, a third part of the rosary ; a religious discourse spoken every evening by the superior to the whole community, called the Spiritual Conference. The day is finished by evening prayer said in common. The prayers then recited are the Lord's Prayer, the Angelical Salutation, the Apostles' Creed. Confession of sinfulness is made by a prayer called the Confiteor ; then acts of faith, hope, and charity, and of contrition, are made. Prayers are then offered up for the dead. In conclusion, the superior gives out the subject for next day's meditation. The rule advises the students to fix their thoughts upon it just before going to sleep, and as soon as they awake.

Twice in the course of the day, when assembled in the chapel, during a pause in the prayers a private examination of conscience is made by each one. The first is made at noon, just before meal time, and is called the particular examination—this means an examination as to the progress made in some virtue specially proposed by each for his own acquisition, or in conquering some vice proposed in the same way for correction. A more general review of conscience for the day is made in the evening.

Each student is required to read a chapter in the Holy Scriptures twice in the day. It would be a departure from the object intended by the rule to spend this time in reading to improve one's self in learning, or to satisfy one's curiosity. The motive here proposed is the quickening of the heart.

It is scarcely necessary to mention prayers at rising and getting into bed, before and after meals, at the ringing of the Angelus, at the beginning and ending of classes, pious aspirations at the sound of the clock, etc., which are common not only to ecclesiastical seminaries but to all Catholic colleges and convent schools.

Mr. Ward quotes his French Informant as stating that the

superior of a seminary must keep his door open to the students at all times. He must "cease to be a man of study. He must give up the notion of being a learned man, otherwise he will not be able to do the good which the diocese expects of him."

I also pass over what the good rector says in regard to the confessions and communions of the students and their selection of a spiritual director. Our Tractarian students at Chelsea, particularly those belonging to the missionary society, were more specially interested at this crisis in what the good French rector said to Mr. Ward about the practice of meditation and spiritual retreats, as used at the seminary. These naturally lead up to that great surprise which the *Ideal of a Christian Church* brought to us, in its account of the "giving of missions."

The most important spiritual exercise noted by the French rector in the list furnished by him to Mr. Ward, as inculcated upon the students by rule, is mental prayer or meditation. This, indeed, is found in all Catholic seminaries. The rector speaks of it in the following terms:

"Mental prayer, or a meditation; in which the student first bows down in adoration before God, acknowledging himself unworthy of keeping himself fixed in his divine presence, and calling upon the Holy Spirit to help him in his meditation. He then enters on the consideration of the subject proposed for meditation, all the while frequently entering into himself, by acts of humiliation, by making good resolutions, and one special good resolve for that very day."

These meditations, with some vocal prayers before and after, are made in the chapel and last half an hour. At the seminaries of St. Sulpice they continue for an hour. This matter of meditation requires some further explanation. Protestants are not easily made to understand what Catholics mean by meditation. And Catholics who have never been Protestants do not know what Protestants mean when they use that word. Among Catholics prayer is generally distinguished into two kinds, oral and mental; but oral prayer is not always uttered according to a prescribed form of words. As a general rule Protestants, whether in public or private prayer, do not follow any set form of words, except when they repeat the Lord's Prayer. Anglicans, indeed, follow a ritual in public worship, and the Common Prayer Book contains a form of prayer for family worship. The general rule, however, is to follow the lead of their own thoughts when praying. Their prayers, indeed, are not meditations. A good memory for thoughts and phrases, coupled with a certain degree of pious excitement, is all that is necessary to furnish a facility for vocal prayer. Nay, more than this, prayer may be purely mental in the sense of being inarticulate, and yet not constitute meditation considered as prayer. When a Protestant minister is said to pray *extempore*, it simply means that he is preaching to his hearers over the divine shoulders. Whatever claim it may have to be called mental prayer, it is by no means meditation. At best, it is only fervent oratory. No doubt private and silent prayer among Protestants does often reach to true prayer of mind and heart. I am not aware, however, that it ever takes that form of systematic study during a set time which is called meditation in the " Exercises " of St. Ignatius, and can be taught to students in a seminary or a convent, or to novices in a religious order.

When, during my course at the seminary in Chelsea, I read Mr. Ward's *Ideal of a Christian Church*, and what the French rector wrote to him concerning mental prayer, I was unable to understand how it could be systematized and taught. I understood it better when, a little later, on my way to the Adirondacks with Bishop Wadhams, then a deacon of the Episcopalian sect, we had for fellow-traveller on the Champlain Canal a young Catholic priest recently ordained in Ireland. We questioned him very closely upon this subject, and, although not apparently a man much given to seclusion or meditation, he was able to give us a very satisfactory account of what he had been taught in regard to the nature of meditation and the means of practising it profitably. The substance of what he told us may be found thoughtfully and beautifully presented in Addis and Arnold's *Catholic Dictionary*, now a familiar book among Catholic Americans :

" Meditation in its narrower and technical sense may be defined as the application of the three powers of the soul to prayer—the memory proposing a religious or moral truth, the understanding considering this truth in its application to the individual who meditates, while the will forms practical resolutions and desires grace to keep them." . . . "The method given by St. Ignatius in his exercise is that generally recommended and used, at least till the person who meditates forms a method of his own."

In truth it may be said that the more thoroughly the habit of mental prayer is acquired the less necessity for the use of method. The "points" selected for meditation become shorter; a single verse of Scripture, a single stanza of a familiar hymn, or indeed a single line or expressive word, furnishes to the soul all the matter needed to start with. A thousand cumulative thoughts cluster around it, the fruit is soon ready to be gathered, holy affections of the heart are sooner reached; holy purposes and resolutions grow up so spontaneously that all thought of method is cast away. The hour or half-hour ceases to be long, until meditation is abandoned for other duties with regret.

I do not stop here to introduce the idea of contemplation, where all process of reasoning ceases and is lost in a sort of passive beholding, a high grade of prayer to which only a few Christians reach.

The French seminary rector quoted in Ward's *Ideal* supposes the nature and purpose of meditation to be well understood, and gives us only the methods to be adopted in order to make it successful and fruitful. A habit of spiritual reading is necessary as the more remote preparation for it. This furnishes the mind with material for thought. To bow down in silence, to call to mind the presence of God, and to invoke the Holy Ghost, are the immediate steps to be taken when beginning this kind of prayer. St. Ignatius intensified its power and extended its influence over souls by introducing his system of spiritual retreats, in which an entire month was given to solitude and meditation. This time is now often shortened to a week, or even three days. These meditations, moreover, were systematized into an admirable series, so arranged that each meditation should naturally lead up to another. The soul is made to consider by turns and progressively the object of its being, its destiny, its sins, the punishment due to sin, the remedies provided through the mercy of God, the means of sanctification through his grace, until at last in this sacred solitude the soul is brought forward to the highest desires for union with its Maker, to the strongest resolves to live for the glory of God alone.

The Catholic Church is furnished with a large number of priests who have trained themselves by long study and careful experience to guide others through these spiritual exercises, as St. Ignatius trained his first companions in the order which he founded.

Finally St. Vincent de Paul began his work of popular missions in country parishes for the benefit of the poor, and especially those most destitute of instruction and spiritual succor. This new form of domestic missionary work has now grown to be almost universal in the Catholic Church, carrying everywhere into the bosom of her fold in a rational way, and with a deeper and fuller power, a reformation of morals and a quickening of spiritual life which the wild emotional efforts of Wesley and Whitefield could not bring about. These missions, regarded in the light of the means and methods employed and the effects produced, may be considered as the natural outgrowth of spiritual retreats. The large audiences gathered cannot be brought to the same solitude and silence, but much of retirement from the world is practically involved in their constant attendance at the church. They cannot meditate as in more private retreats, but an unusual amount of reflection is involved in listening to so many daily sermons and instructions, and taking so much part in prayer. Skilful missionaries consult together upon the order of subjects to be introduced. The confessional shows how far the good seed sown has produced good results and what is still most wanting, and both the order of preaching and the special way of treating each sermon may be varied accordingly. In fine, the method of "giving missions" has grown to be a peculiar science and holy art unknown outside of the Catholic Church.

All the above is introduced in this place as belonging to these reminiscences of a Protestant seminary at a most momen-

tous period.   We seminarians at Chelsea were all of us more or
less interested in a great attempt to galvanize Anglicanism.
Ward's new book introduced us to Romanism, so called, as fur-
nishing the best practical ideal of a true Christian Church.
One prominent sign of its vitality lay in its wonder-working
custom and method of giving missions. His book gave a description of a mission furnished to him by a prominent Roman
Catholic, with most interesting details of its purpose, plan, and
effects.   It was a new light.   Mr. Ward's book is not accessible
to me at this moment, and perhaps it is not necessary at this
time to introduce any extracts from it. Suffice it to say that
for the most part the conduct of these missions is left to missionaries reared in convents. To this circumstance is due in
some degree the fact that many of us students, when looking
forward to our own career in the ministry, were led to associate
monasticism with our aspirations to a life of missionary labor.

CHAPTER VII.

SLOWNESS OF THE MOVEMENT ROMEWARD.—OVER HASTY AT-
TEMPTS TO CRACK THE PROTESTANT NUT.—DUNIGAN.—
BAKER. — PHINNEY. — MOEHLER'S "SYMBOLISM."—LIVES OF
THE EARLY ENGLISH SAINTS.

CATHOLICS whose attention had been called to the novelties brewing at our seminary must have thought it very
strange that it took us so long to find out where the truth
lay and to embrace the whole Catholic faith, worship, and church
with one confiding hug. It needs but a short argument to
show that only the Catholic body has true unity and that
variation is the very law and life of Protestantism. This ought
to be enough to bring them all into the true fold by a short
and easy process. Men who think thus, however, think so very
superficially. In real life the best and most earnest minds are
not accustomed to travel by these short cuts. An extensive
horse-breeder and trainer once said, in answer to a question of
mine: "Horses, sir, are very intelligent animals, and when they
see an old charred stump on the roadside they know very
well that it's nothing but a stump. But you see they are very
cautious creatures; nature has made them so, and they don't
know at first sight what is behind the stump."

It was the same thing with many of us at the seminary.
We soon got used to discussions about the church. We soon
learned to understand that Christ instituted a visible church,
organized a tangible and approachable body. That church he
officered himself, giving it not only a complete doctrine to
transmit, and sacraments furnished with grace, but also a
divine mission, or right to act in his name. This right, we
understood, could only be transmitted by that church and in it.
This mission or divine current of jurisdiction is interrupted by
schism and ceases to flow into a severed member. All this was

pretty much understood by the more advanced Tractarian students at the seminary, and yet they were by no means prepared to leap at once into the ancient church. Other questions, profound and precious, lay before them still unsolved. Let me here refer to an incident which occurred at some time during my second year at the seminary, precisely when I cannot remember, which exemplifies how hard it is for Catholics " to the manner born " to understand the perplexities and needs of a Protestant outsider searching for the truth.

I went down-street one day to Dunigan's bookstore. He kept at that time, if I remember right, far down in Broadway, or possibly in William or Nassau Street. I inquired for Moehler's *Symbolism*. He said to me (I think it was Dunigan himself) :

" I don't think it is Moehler that you want."

" What then do I want ? " I returned.

" The right book for you," he said, " is Bossuet's *Variations of Protestantism.*"

" No, sir. You are mistaken. The variations of Protestantism have been going on since Bossuet died, and perhaps I know of many variations that he never heard of."

" Ah," said he, " I think I understand you. What you need is Milner's *End of Controversy.* That's something quite recent."

" No," I persisted, " I do not need Milner either. I read it through and through, and feel no call to refer to it any more. I know its contents pretty well and have gathered much truth out of it, but it is not the end of controversy for me. I have other questions to solve and deeper ones. What I want is Moehler's *Symbolism.*"

He gave me a compassionate smile, but found the book for me and I took it home to my room in the seminary. It proved to be a treasure indeed. I think I learned of the existence and contents of this book from some reference or review of it in the *British Critic.* It had made a deep impression on Dr. Newman's mind.

Protestants are not heathens ; far from it. Their reasons cannot be reached by the same easy and simple means which suffice for the ignorant heathen. When the Christian revelation is fairly presented to the heathen mind, their ignorance has so little to show in opposition that they are more ready to embrace it trustfully and in its entirety. The obex, or obstacle, to truth presented by their simple superstitions is a comparatively small one. The Protestant mind, on the contrary, however cultivated, is by no means simple, nor in the same sense ignorant. It is nearer the truth to say that they know too much. They are oftentimes, to quote St. Paul, "more wise than it behoveth to be wise." Their minds are too much possessed with things that are not so. The obex which they present to Catholic truth is something multitudinous, complex, over-refined. It is so engrafted, so commingled with their pious emotions, so closely webbed and interwoven with all their past thoughts and memories, that they mistake prejudice for a rational conviction. True doctrine "in a nutshell" is not truth presented in a form in which they can receive it. The attempt so frequently made thus to present it, and settle the whole question at once, is well illustrated in my memory by an anecdote from the experience of Father Baker, the Paulist, which I have from himself. During the time when he was stationed as rector at St. Luke's Church, Baltimore, a priest rang the bell at his door and asked to see him. He presented no card and gave no name. Baker's sister, who opened the door, noticing this and not liking the exterior make-up of the visitor, whose language and style of dress were something new to her, was somewhat alarmed and disinclined to introduce him to her brother's room. This, however, she did. He took his seat and immediately opened the purpose of his visit. What he said was substantially as follows:

"I have heard of you, Mr. Baker. I understand that you have strong inclinations toward the Catholic Church, but you remain still in doubt. I can prove to you in a few short words that she is the only true church. Now listen to me attentively for a moment. See here! The church is necessarily one, for Christ her founder is one, and he only made one. Keep that in mind. Now then: the church is also holy, for Christ made her so, in order to sanctify the world. Keep that in mind also." He

Your affectionate friend.
Francis A Baker.

then proceeded in like manner to show that the true church must be Catholic and apostolic. After this, in the same brief manner, he went on to prove that only the Roman Catholic Church bore these four marks of being the true one. Father Baker listened in silence to what he had to say, but was quite surprised to see the good father rise after completing this short argument; a hearty shaking of hands followed, and satisfied with this the enthusiastic visitor withdrew, feeling that he had finished his job. He was a good man and a most exemplary priest. He belonged to a class of men to be met with every-where. Wadhams and I heard of him during the course of this year, or the winter of the next, while among the Adirondacks. McMaster had been visited by him in his retirement at Hyde Park, and had been highly pleased by him, for this priest had seen much, and there were few places in the United States which he had not visited; he knew something of everything. He came to me shortly after I became a Catholic and proposed to me a variety of good devotions. I did not care to be ham-pered with too many things all at once, and in this I was sup-ported by the counsel of a wise director. Such men do not generally bring about many healthy conversions. But if treated wisely and gently by their superiors, and not trusted with the management of difficult matters, they may do more good than wiser men with less worthy motives.

I fear to have set down too strong an example to illustrate well the point I would present. Many Catholics even with bet-ter regulated minds often make serious mistakes when under-taking to lead converts into the church.

The false maxims to which Protestants have become accus-tomed may be digested and generalized, and so briefly stated as to find room in a nutshell. That nutshell, however, they will never acknowledge. They know that in their hearts there is a religion deeper, truer, and more solid than that nut holds. You may crack that nut before their eyes, but they do not feel hurt by your vigorous hammer.

A little more than three years after leaving the seminary at Chelsea I happened to be in Birmingham, England. The Rev. Dr. Phinney, of Oberlin College, was there at the same time

preaching; I had got acquainted with him some six years earlier when in the United States. I admired the man and felt
much attached to him. Another gentleman, whose acquaintance
I had made in America, was also in Birmingham at the same
time; this was Baron Schroeder, a highly educated Catholic
layman from Germany. He persuaded me to go with him on a
visit to Dr. Phinney at his lodgings. Dr. Phinney and his wife
received us both very cordially and we had a long and pleasant
interview. A good part of the time was spent in amicable controversy. I was, of course, but a novice in theology. The
baron was a well-educated scholar, especially in philosophy.
Professor Phinney, intellectually far superior to either of us, was
not only an eloquent and powerful preacher, but an expert in
doctrinal discussion. I only introduce this visit here to illustrate what I have said, that Protestantism, if it be understood
to comprise all that constitutes the religious life and belief of an
earnest Protestant, cannot be reduced to the compass of a nutshell.

"Gentlemen," said the good doctor in the course of conversation, "I am not prepared to say that I hold no religious errors. Some of these may possibly be important errors. One
thing, however, I cannot allow myself to admit. To allow that
I do not understand the Christian religion in its substantial and
essential features is a supposition from which my whole soul re-
coils."

I give Dr. Phinney as a type of an earnest and intelligent
Protestant. There was a vast amount of belief in him. No
nutshell could cover it.

Moehler had studied well the age in which he lived. He knew
the Protestant mind. He knew that it could not be captured
by a single syllogism, and that a few texts establishing church
authority are seldom sufficient to bring an educated Protestant
to the true faith and into the true fold. Moehler devotes his
book on symbolism not only to these but to all the doctrines
which belong to religious faith and worship. He treats of the
attributes of God, the nature of man, man's relations with God,
the nature of grace, etc. He compares together carefully the
acknowledged symbols of Protestantism and Catholicity, and
presents both in their real light to religious souls who wish to

live by the true law of spiritual life. Such Protestants are the only ones that come to the Catholic Church, or at least that come to stay. Catholic polemics in our day must learn new texts of Scripture, glean new maxims from the Christian fathers, and provide new fish-hooks and more efficient bait. So far as I know of, no convert of the Chelsea Seminary was brought to the door of the Catholic Church either by Milner's *End of Controversy* or Bossuet's *Variations,* strong though they be.

The general spirit which characterized that seminary was, to the best of my recollection and in my opinion, a good one. There was a value attached to sound doctrine, and very little attached to the idea that " it makes little difference what a man believes, if only he be sincere." Dogmatic theology—that is to say, the science of presenting religious truth in its true aspect and in its proper relations with other truths—stood high in honor there. I cannot remember that I ever heard dogmatic theology spoken of respectfully until I came to the seminary at Chelsea. Religion and all that is worth knowing about religion is generally supposed by Protestants to come to one as Santa Claus comes to the children, while they are not looking out for it, but asleep.

Our Tractarian students at Chelsea ranked high among the others as diligent scholars, and this gained for them favor with the professors, the majority of whom were by no means Tractarian. It is not to be wondered at that students of this stamp when once introduced to Moehler's *Symbolism,* should become fascinated with it. It was not a book which professed to teach Catholicity in six easy lessons which should avoid all necessity of investigating farther. It did not profess to furnish an all-sufficient egg which should develop itself and required no brooding to bring it to a development. Moehler takes up the whole of Catholic doctrine, yet article by article. The external marks of the true church, which prove her right to teach, are not omitted. The doctrines which she teaches are also all brought forward and have their own distinct grounds to stand upon. The acknowledged councils of the church with her canons and decrees when cited are given in her own words, not fearing to commit her to her own declarations. Side by side with these

are placed the doctrines of the Protestant reformers, expressed
in their own words. The Anglican Church, with her symbols
or formularies of doctrine and worship, is placed side by side
with the Roman Catholic, as the queen in " Hamlet " is made to
look first at the portrait of her husband and then upon the face
of her crowned paramour—

"Look here, upon this picture, and on this."

Moehler understands well the effect necessarily produced upon a fair mind by two faithful portraits thus distinctly presented
in their own dress and with their own native features. Then
the beholder with a genuine conviction may say of the true
king—

"See, what a grace was seated on this brow,"

while the other has little but his clothing to present, and stands

" A king of shreds and patches!"

a mere show of apostolical succession, without any rightful in-
heritance of divine mission, holding forth a Common Prayer
Book which comprises in one cover a jumbled jargon of doctrine.

Moehler's *Symbolism* did more to lead me to a comprehensive
knowledge of the Catholic faith and to take the final step of
entering the Catholic fold than any other book. I have always
preferred it above all others as a book to lend to thoughtful
and studious Protestants.

I have perhaps said enough to show what doctrinal vitality—
that is, what eagerness to know the real truth—existed among
Episcopalians at the time included in these reminiscences, and
was perhaps more focused at our seminary than anywhere else in
America. It would be a great oversight to make no mention of
a spirit still more precious and vital which I found kindled there
and which must account for many conversions to the faith.
Arthur Carey was the chief centre of this flame, as he was the
chief leader in the inquiry after truth. His residence at the
seminary occupied a period of four years, including one year

during which, being too young for ordination, he kept his old room, mingling as freely with the students as a secluded life of study and prayer like his would allow. Every one was glad to know him, even those who looked upon him as all the more dangerous from the very fact of his being pious, sincere, and virtuous. His sayings about religious topics of the day were repeated about among us from mouth to mouth, as the last words would be cited that came from Newman or Dalgairns. Not all were disposed to follow his opinions, but no one could afford to be ignorant of what he thought and said. It cannot reasonably be doubted that at the bottom of the Tractarian movement there lay, not merely a demand for pure and Catholic truth but also for a holy life. The spirit of high and dry churchmanship did not preside at the seminary. It was, no doubt, the real spirit of Anglicanism, but it was as unpalatable to Tractarians as it was to Evangelicals, and more so.

In this state of things it was impossible that books emanating from Oxford, and showing the new kindled piety which breathed there, should not find free circulation at the seminary. Keble's *Christian Year* lay here and there upon the tables of those who loved poetry. Soon followed the *Lyra Apostolica*, to which Keble, Newman, Hurrell Froude, and many other leading spirits of the "Movement" contributed words burning with piety and often radiant with the truest poetry. Faber was better known at that time as a romantic poet, but he was recognized "as one of them," and as such found a few readers amongst us. But a greater charm than any of these possessed was to be found in the *Lives of the Early English Saints.* This was a series of biographies written by Anglicans of the Oxford school, and was a most influential element in its great movement towards real Catholic truth and life. The series was confined to English saints. There was wisdom in this restriction. It took into account English national prejudice by showing lives of sanctity lived on English ground. At the same time an honest presentation of English sanctity in early times would be sure to show how little it looks like modern Anglican piety, and how distinctly it presents itself associated with the doctrines, worship, and austere practices of the Church

of Rome. The writers of these lives did not propose, nor indeed consciously intend, to lead their readers to relinquish their
own communion and unite with the Roman Catholics. What
they proposed is well stated by Wilfrid Ward in his book entitled *William George Ward and the Oxford Movement* (chapter
vii. page 142). He says :

"The love of Rome and of an united Christendom which
marked the new school was not purely a love for ecclesiastical
authority. This was indeed one element; but there was another
yet more influential in many minds—admiration for the saints of
the Roman Church, and for the saintly ideal as realized especially in the monastic life. We have already seen how this
element operated in Mr. Ward's own history. Froude had
struck the note of sanctity as well as the note of authority.
He had raised an inspiring ideal on both heads; and behold,
with however much of practical corruption and superstition
mixed up with their practical exhibition, these ideals were
actually reverenced, attempted, often realized, in the existing
Roman Church. The worthies of the English Church—even
when sharing the tender piety of George Herbert or Bishop
Ken—fell short of the heroic aims, the martial sanctity, gained
by warfare unceasing against world, flesh, and devil, which they
found exhibited in Roman Hagiology. The glorying in the
cross of Christ which is the key-note to such lives as those of
St. Ignatius of Loyola and St. Francis Xavier, while it recalled
much in the life of St. Paul, had no counterpart in post-Re-
formation Anglicanism."

As early as the long vacation at Oxford of 1842 the idea
suggested itself to the mind of Dr. Newman of getting out
this series of the Lives of the English Saints, and immediate
measures were taken to secure writers and prepare for publication. The first of the series reached our seminary, I think, in
the winter of 1843 and '44, during my second year's course. I
have no complete list by me of the saints comprised in this
series, but it included the Life of St. Stephen Harding, founder
of the Cistercians, which involves much of that of his disciple,
the great St. Bernard, St. Austin of Canterbury, St. Woolstan,
St. William, St. Paulinus, St. Bega, St. Gilbert, St. Richard and

his family, and Legends of Hermit Saints, some of these written by Newman himself.

These biographies were couched in language more or less watered to suit Anglican ears; but no daintiness of style nor dilution of matter could conceal the fact that the early English saints were utterly unlike Anglicans of the present day. In his *Apologia pro Vita Sua* Dr. Newman gives us his motives for starting this new enterprise.

" I thought it would be useful," he says, " as employing the minds of men who were in danger of running wild, bringing them from doctrine to history, and from speculation to fact ; again, as giving them an interest in the English soil and the English Church, and keeping them from seeking sympathy in Rome, as she is ; and further as seeking to promote the spread of right views."

This plan, however, for holding back earnest and truth-seeking minds from the necessary consequences which attach to truth, could not and did not work. Scarcely had his project taken wing than he was forced to write to a friend : " Within the last month, it has come upon me that, if the scheme goes on, it will be a practical carrying out of No. 90 ; from the character of the usages and opinions of ante-reformation times."

So indeed it was. Like No. 90, it forced matters onward to a crisis both in England and America. It did more than this. It led many eager minds to a more special consideration of monastic life as combining in its bosom a special grace for self-purification and perfection with a zeal for missionary labor. St. Stephen Harding, of Citeaux, was the model of a monk to whom the whole world had nothing to offer. St. Bernard, his great disciple, carried out from Citeaux a burning heart to which the world of souls was always appealing.

In the next chapter I propose to show how the admiration for monasticism thus aroused led ardent souls among the Chelsea graduates and students to projecting monastic institutions in their own church and actually experimenting in them.

CHAPTER VIII.

THE last three chapters show how Tractarian doctrines, so
rife at the Chelsea Seminary, acting upon a spirit of interior piety and zeal for the salvation of souls, and combining
both of these together in the same bosoms, led on gradually
to an eagerness to introduce something like monastic life into
Anglicanism.   Americans are a people too practical and enterprising to be much attracted by thumb-sucking saints.   Even our
transcendental pantheists of New England, inclined as they are
betimes to contemplation and fond of Brahminical lore and
legends, are not easily disposed to sit dreaming with their backs
against the trunks of trees until their hair grows into the bark.
At Brook Farm the stirring motto was

> Hast thou aught to teach, then teach it ;
> Preach it
>   Loud and long ;
>   Sing it if it be a song.
> Be thou prophet, be thou poet,
> If thou know it, go it—
>   Strong.

When Dalgairns's *Life of St. Stephen Harding* first found its
way across the water to Chelsea, the sensation it produced was
intense.   St. Bernard was not an Englishman, and his character
and career could not easily be put forth directly in a series of
Lives of the English Saints.   But St. Stephen, the founder of
Citeaux, could give his name to a volume which should bring

forward luminously the career of the great St. Bernard, the master-spirit of the Cistercian Order. St. Bernard was one of the very holiest of contemplatives; and yet, forced from the seclusion which he loved by his burning zeal, by the constant needs and pressing calls of Christendom, his voice was made to resound throughout the whole Continent of Europe. He was, in truth, the very type of a missionary monk.

Something like Citeaux was already existing in the Anglican Church of America. It was at Nashotah, in Wisconsin. This institute was in reality an attempt, under the name of a missionary station, to found a veritable monastery. Its founder was James Lloyd Breck, a graduate of the Chelsea Seminary of 1841. Associated with him were two of his classmates, William Adams and John Henry Hobart. That the intention was to found a monastery is evident from a letter, now in my possession, written by Breck to Wadhams, October 21, 1842, inviting him to come and join them. The letter says:

" If, dear Wadhams, you conclude to come, remember we receive you on the ground of our first principles, which are: (1) so long as connected with this institution to remain unmarried; (2) to yield implicit and full obedience to all the rules and regulations of the body; (3) community of goods so long as community of purpose; (4) teaching on the staunch Catholic principles; (5) preaching from place to place on circuits—route, mode, etc., to be determined by the bishop, or by one authorized by him."

An earlier letter to the same from Adams breathes the same spirit. "Dear brother," he writes, "if you can in almost every way deny yourself, can be content to remain unmarried for an indefinite period, to live on the coarsest food, to deny yourself the pleasure of cultivated society; then come to Wisconsin."

As Nashotah, then an object of longing interest to many hearts at the General Seminary, grew in a few years to be a flourishing institution, though far different from what its founders intended to make it, it may be well to give some further description of this institute and its locality, in its early days. Bishop Kip, of California, visited it as early as 1847. I gather the following materials from a pamphlet of his, published at that time, entitled *A few Days at Nashotah.* The lands of the

Nashotah Mission were adjoining those of Bishop Kemper, then having charge of the territory in which this mission was included. On their first arrival Breck, Adams, and Hobart had assigned to them Prairieville, with a circuit of thirty miles around. After nine months they settled at the Nashotah Lakes. Bishop Kip thus describes their location :

" The whole of this part of the country is intersected by the most beautiful lakes, so that from a hill a few miles distant eleven can be counted in sight, while more than double that number can be found in a circle of twelve miles. They are of various sizes, the largest being about two miles in length—some dotted with islands—the water perfectly clear, and the shore generally a high bluff, rising many feet above the surface. Two of these, which approach within a hundred feet of each other, and are united by a little brook, have retained the Indian name of *Nashotah,* or *Twin Lakes.* On the bank of one of them, where the shore rises fifty feet above the water, and then spreads out into a level *plateau,* covered with oak-trees standing in clumps (an oak opening), are the mission buildings." Across this lake and on a small prairie are remarkable Indian mounds, twelve feet high. One represents a tortoise, another a serpent, another a bear. Large trees grow on some of them, showing great age.

In 1847, when Kip wrote, the institution had grown from the one-story log-house, described in my Reminiscences of Bishop Wadhams, to eight or ten low wooden buildings, and he tells us that " The view from this spot is probably one of the most enchanting that the world can furnish."

Breck, formerly at St. Paul's College, Flushing, L. I., had been a pupil of the Rev. Dr. Muhlenberg, whose beautiful church on the corner of Twentieth Street and Fifth Avenue, New York City, was building in 1843, and eagerly watched by us seminarians. We looked upon the worthy doctor as neither low nor high nor dry, but as a true Catholic in our romantic sense of the word. He was particularly a favorite among students of the ritualistic type. He was admired then as a poet, with a keen taste for church architecture, author of the beautiful hymn, " I would not live alway," now known also as the founder of St. Luke's Hospital, under the care of Episcopalian nuns. The Paulists in Fifty-ninth Street have a beautiful crucifixion by Guido, as a testimonial of gratitude to Father Deshon from Dr. Muhlenberg, for helping to guard his hospital during the draft riot in 1863.

Muhlenberg was visiting Breck's institute when Kip was there. At that time the washing of the institution was done by students for poverty's sake. They had also a baptistery there; *i. e.*, "a flight of steps leading into the water at a convenient depth for immersion, where a platform has been placed on the bottom." Bishop Kip gives as a reason for this, that many of the settlers around were Baptists; but from what I know of Breck, and that strong yearning existing then as now among Anglicans for some show of union with those happy Oriental Greek churches which practise immersion, they would have done the same thing if these modern Anabaptists had migrated further westward. Bishop Kip gives us the mode of immersion at Nashotah, which, he says, is different from the way in which it is performed among the Baptists (*i. e.*, more genteel), where the individual is immersed backwards. Here he kneels in the water, the officiating priest places one hand behind his head, and, taking him at the same time by the hand, bends him forward till the immersion is complete, and then aids him in rising.

In addition to the practice of poverty, celibacy, and obedience, which, as we have seen, Breck and Adams announced to Wadhams as requirements of their institute, the principle attached to monasticism since the time of the earliest hermits and cenobites of the desert, that labor must be associated with prayer, was carried out after some fashion at Nashotah as late as Bishop Kip's visit. He tells us that during the summer vacation, which lasted from the middle of June to the middle of November, the studies were suspended and the students labored eight hours a day. Many of these were in the harvest-field, where they were seen by Kip at work. "We found," said he, "about a dozen employed in getting in the wheat, on a tract which had been cleared and brought into cultivation since the mission was established." I find no account of contemplative prayer as filling up the hours not occupied by labor or study, but a routine of life is given in which appear hours for chapel service, with days for receiving communion, etc., as in ordinary seminaries and colleges.

This whole mission of Bishop Kemper, with the bishop's house and seminary at Nashotah for its centre, was the carrying out of a scheme to draw Episcopalian emigration and to colonize and Anglicanize the emigrants. It much resembles Archbishop Ireland's more recent colonization plan for Minnesota, and, like that plan, was eminently successful. The plan of the Nashotah plant contemplated at one and the same time colonization, missionary labor, and monastic life. The first two parts of this plan have succeeded wonderfully well. The success of the last was very short; love got into the tub and the bottom fell out.

This Nashotah property was held by the Rev. James Lloyd Breck, in trust, for the education of students both theological and academical. In 1841 they had one student. This number had increased at the time when Kip visited it, in 1847, to twenty-three students. At that time the members of the mission had seventeen stations for preaching and lay reading, within a circuit of thirty miles. The students acted as lay readers and catechists among the emigrants of the neighborhood. The idea of the three founders was to establish an institution which should be essentially monastic. The bishop humored this idea, for Breck and his companions were valuable men, and, however visionary their special hopes might be, it would have been a dangerous thing to discourage them. The letters of Breck and Adams from which we have selected short extracts, but which are given at greater length in the Reminiscences of Bishop Wadhams, show the eager anxiety for celibacy and monastic life which reigned in the bosoms of the writers. But the aim of Bishop Kemper is better disclosed by his friend, Dr. Kip, who writes not only to recommend the institution to the patronage of Episcopalians generally, but takes care to excuse and explain away certain apparent tendencies to Romanism which hover about the place. Dr. Kip writes:

"One of the most common charges against the institution is, that the doctrine of the *celibacy of the clergy* is inculcated.

We take, therefore, this opportunity to deny it. Such is not the case. The only foundation for the story is, that a student upon joining the institution pledges himself not to form any engagement with reference to matrimony during his union with it. The moment he is ordained he is, of course, left free to do as he pleases. We believe that there is no one acquainted with the state of things in some other seminaries of our church but must feel that it would be better for the students if they were under the restriction of this rule. If there was less visiting, there would be more theology."

Dr. Kip's pleasant way of waving off the charges and suspicions against Nashotah agree as little with my own remembrances of the time as they do with Breck's own letters. I was one of several candidates for orders whose missionary aspirations blending with the love of solitude and a yearning for the graces attached to a spiritual life in the cloister drew me strongly to Nashotah, and I applied to my father for permission to join that institution and finish my studies there. But the rumors above mentioned had reached his ears and made him hesitate. He consulted Dr. Horatio Potter, afterward Bishop of New York, and then rector of St. Peter's Church in Albany. Dr. Potter advised him by no means to consent to it, as Puseyism reigned there in its worst forms. This ended the matter for me. Bishop Kemper utilized the zeal and labors of Breck and his Tractarian friends, but all for his own purposes, not for theirs. Breck's airy vision soon melted away like a mist.

Hobart left Nashotah in its infancy to take a wife. Six of its early students, finding that its monastic character was nothing but a thin garment cautiously tolerated by authority and for a present purpose only, broke away from the delusion to unite with the Catholic Church. Three of these, McCurry, Graves, and Robinson, visited me at St. Peter's Church, Troy, in 1859, the time of their emancipation. McCurry, by my advice, attached himself to the diocese of Albany, and upon his ordination was appointed assistant priest in St. John's Church, in Albany City. A vacancy occurring in the church at Cooperstown, he was sent there to supply the place temporarily, and died there. He was a most valuable and pious priest. Graves also took or-

ders in the Catholic Church, connecting himself with one of the
Wisconsin dioceses.   Robinson was rector of the Church of
the Holy Name of Jesus, at Chicopee, Mass., but within the
last few months he died.

Although John Henry Hobart's connection with Nashotah
was so brief, yet the fact of his being a graduate of the Chelsea Seminary, with a memory still fresh in its halls, when I arrived there, as a forward Tractarian, the son of an illustrious
bishop and himself remarkable for high personal qualifications,
seems to demand further notice in these Reminiscences. I saw
him and conversed with him only twice. The first time was at
Saratoga Springs. It must have been, I think, in the summer
of 1844. My object was to obtain such information as I might
concerning the community and life at Nashotah. His answers
to my inquiries impressed me very much in his favor as a young
man of unusual intelligence, honorable feeling, and refined courtesy. He spoke frankly of the Nashotah Institute and of his
former companions, Breck and Adams. His statements concerning the institute were always highly favorable, and of his friends
there he spoke with much regard and affection. He did not
attempt to make the least defence of his act in leaving them.

"You must not expect me, Mr. Walworth, to offer any excuse for my action," he said, "beyond my own weakness and
instability of purpose. My companions were too noble and
spiritual for me. Their vocation is a higher one than mine, and
cheerfully will I recommend this community to any young man
who can keep pace with such spirits as Breck and Adams, and
make such sacrifices as they make. So far as I am concerned
the public will be my judges, and will, no doubt, judge rightly."

There was a truthfulness and dignity in this frank and simple confession of weakness which, to my mind at the time,
amounted to sublimity. I thought I saw in it a generosity
of nature which made him worthy of his distinguished father
and of his noble-minded sister, the convert-wife of Dr. Levi Sil-
liman Ives, who became more distinguished as a Catholic layman than he had been as Protestant bishop. He was near kinsman, moreover, to Mother Seton, foundress of Emmittsburg,
the mother-house of the Sisters of Charity in this country; a

kinsman, too, of James Roosevelt Bayley, who died Archbishop of Baltimore. Every soul is precious in the eyes of God. Is it an ill-directed sentiment to feel sad that a gifted young man, so connected with converts to the true church, should have died without its pale? His death occurred in 1889. He was assistant minister of Trinity Church, New York City.

Following Hobart's advice, I visited the Rev. Mr. Tucker, now and for many years past rector of Holy Cross Church, in Troy, well known as founded through the charity of Mrs. Warren of that city. Tucker was a graduate of Chelsea, well known there to us both and thoroughly intimate with Breck and Adams. I have no distinct recollection of my interview with Tucker except that it was a very pleasant one, and that he was well posted in what concerned Nashotah, of which institute he was a warm advocate.

The next time that I saw Hobart was also at Saratoga Springs, after I had become a Catholic. He was not at all surprised, nor did he express the least regret. I myself should not have felt the least surprise at that time had I heard of his doing the same thing, although in such a case, having matrimony in view, he would have been obliged, like Dr. Ives, his brother-in-law, to live as a layman.

Adams was a better school-master than he was pioneer or monk. Breck's deeper spirituality and greater energy were in the beginning far more valuable in drawing zealous young Tractarians to what promised to be a life of mortification, devotion, and missionary enterprise. Bishop Kemper knew well how to avail himself of such qualities without letting his horse run away with him. As time advanced, however, students gathered and emigrants fell into line. This brought into greater prominence and gave more comparative value to the scholarly qualities and more sedentary habits of Adams. The institute at Nashotah shaped itself more and more to the ordinary wants and ways of an Episcopalian seminary and college, while playing monk became more of a nuisance to all interested parties, who really cared nothing for monk or cowl.

Adams soon took a wife. What special circumstances led to this I cannot tell, but it is a fact of history that Cupid smiled upon him in the form of his own bishop's daughter. His vocation became thus settled. He is still a professor at the Nashotah Seminary, his department being that of Systematic Divinity.

Mr. E. C. Arnold, a convert, now public librarian at Taunton, Mass., and once a bookseller at Milwaukee, was quite familiar with Nashotah in its early years. I have from him the following account of Breck's subsequent career:

"Adams's marriage to Bishop Kemper's daughter was a great grief to Breck, and as he felt unable to cope with the 'married influence,' he eventually turned his back on Nashotah and started a similar institution at Faribault, Minn. While there he paid Bishop Grace several visits, and we sent him books from Milwaukee; but ere long he got entangled matrimonially himself, and that put an end to his earlier dreams."

His last station was in California. He died rector of St. Paul's Church, Benicia, in that State. One monument to the busy life of this remarkable man is found in the "Breck Mission and Farm School," Wilder, Minnesota.

The only other attempt to introduce monasticism into the Episcopalian Church in the United States in which I took part, or of which I have any personal recollections, was a scheme which originated also at the General Seminary in the City of New York. The central figure in this scheme was Edgar P. Wadhams, a graduate of the class of 1843, who received deacon's orders immediately after graduation and was put in charge of the whole of Essex County. I suppose I must name myself as the second figure in the plan, since I was the only one of the cenobites that actually located himself at the proposed scene of operations, which was the village of Wadhams' Mills, in the old homestead of that family. Our actual community consisted of two, Deacon Wadhams and myself. We occupied the second story of the house, Widow Wadhams presiding over the lower story. Our flat (the convent which we dedicated to St. Mary) comprised two large rooms with hall and stairway. The room at the south end was the convent kitchen, with a bed for my accommodation. The room at the north end, a very large one, was at once the larder, general store-room, lumber loft, and carpenter's working shop. Wadhams occupied a small bed-chamber on the first floor, there being no place for him in the cloister above. Our chapel, to which we had no

EDGAR P. WADHAMS AS BISHOP OF OGDENSBURG.

claim except on Sundays, was the village school-house. On Christmas we celebrated Episcopalian Mass in Widow Wadhams' parlor which was richly decorated for the occasion with evergreens. We had no other common oratory than the community kitchen; the stove, cupboard, dining-table, bed, and washstand harmonizing sufficiently well with our simple devotions. For brevity's sake I may call this our Chapter-House. Here also Wadhams and I had our spiritual readings when we two were alone. Sometimes, however, to please Widow Wadhams, this exercise was held in her kitchen, for she loved to assist at these readings when she could, especially when we read from the Lives of the Saints. Alban Butler's simple " Lives " delighted her especially. On these occasions two of her grandsons, children of William Wadhams, a Presbyterian deacon, assisted, for they lodged and boarded with their grandmother. The kitchen-girl also could not always be absent, unless she stayed outdoors. A stranger could not easily have distinguished, even in the premises outside the house, between the cloister and the world. The cow-house was under the jurisdiction of the convent, for Prior Wadhams owned the cow, and I kept her apartments clean for her " with my spade and shovel "; and I kept the cow. Prior Wadhams also owned a pony named *Beni*, who was lodged on the other side of the highway, in the stable of Deacon William Wadhams. All the other out buildings belonged to Mrs. Wadhams, with all the pigs, hens, ducks, geese, turkeys, and doves that occupied or frequented them.

This location of our monastery was only a temporary one. About a mile distant to the northward lay a beautiful tract of land, where a large creek, after tumbling down from among the Adirondack Mountains, made a wide sweep around an extensive farm of meadow backed by woodland, then headed directly for the little village or corners named Wadhams' Mills, passing close behind our house, to leap over a fine fall and supply water for the village mill. Our future hopes were all centred in the farm just mentioned. It was the hereditary property of our prior. On it we saw in the dim future a noble monastic pile giving shelter and seclusion to a cowled community of contemplatives, missionaries, scholars, and a thousand other visionary things of religious dream-land. This vision melted away in the next spring-time, leaving nothing but a log hut that never received either community or roof. Our monastic pile, if it still remains, is only a pile of logs.

My memory recalls no fruitful experiments among Episcopalians to found monastic communities of men. Religious communities of women have had better success. The reader will remember that when Dr. Kip visited Nashotah he there met the Rev. Dr. Muhlenberg on a similar visit. It may be that the latter had already at that time some enthusiastic predilection for monasticism. The first introduction of religious sisterhoods amongst Episcopalians in this country that I remember was when Dr. Muhlenberg, of New York, put St. Luke's Hospital under charge of such women. Similar sisterhoods are now not at all unfrequent. A boarding-school for young ladies, named Kemper Hall, now exists at Kenosha, Wisconsin, under charge of ladies of this kind. They are called the Sisters of St. Mary. Other sisters bearing the same title are found at Memphis, Tenn.; Peekskill, N. Y.; Islip, L. I.; Rockaway Beach, and at six different locations in New York City. These seem to belong to one general order, the time of first foundation reaching back as far as 1865. Besides these, other Episcopalian societies of religious ladies are to be found bearing various titles, such as the following: The Sisters of the Good Shepherd, of the Holy Communion, of the Holy Child Jesus, of St. John the Evangelist, of SS. Philip and James, All Saints' Sisters of the Poor, Colored Sisters of St. Mary and All Saints, Sisters of St. Martha, of the Holy Nativity, of the Holy Name, of St. Monica. They are located at New York, Albany, St. Louis, Brooklyn, New Orleans, Baltimore, Louisville, Providence, Tyler in Texas, and Fond du Lac, Wis.

Some of these are branches of conventual institutes of the Church of England; for example, that of St. John Baptist, New York; that of St. Margaret, Boston; that of All Saints' Sisters of the Poor, Baltimore. So far as I know, and as I believe, all these sisters are considered as nuns. They wear some fashion of religious habit and are not easily to be distinguished at sight from Catholic sisters, except that their eyes are not much cloistered, and that their gait and walk have not received any apparent modification since they put off their secular dress.

The Church Almanac and Year Book for 1892 exhibits an existing and recognized order of deaconesses. What they are I cannot tell; whether they are nuns or not, nor when they first became a feature of Episcopalianism. They are specially educated to their work, one training-school being in New York and one in Philadelphia. A still older one, called the Church Home, has existed in Mobile since 1863.

To what extent the vows of poverty, chastity, and obedience are enjoined amongst these Protestant nuns is more than I can tell. I remember, however, that when Dr. Muhlenberg introduced his Sisters into St. Luke's Hospital it was said that their vocation was cemented by vows, and that the vow of chastity consisted in an obligation to remain single until it should please God to call them to some other state of life. One thing should be set down as undoubted; that no part of all this tendency toward the monastic life is an outcrop of Protestantism, but must be attributed to the Tractarian movement.

CHAPTER IX.

AFTER EFFECTS OF CAREY'S ORDINATION.—WAR ON BISHOP ON-
DERDONK IN DIOCESAN CONVENTION.—THE BISHOP'S MAS-
TERLY DEFENCE.—JUDGE DUER'S SPEECH.—A CHANGE OF
TACTICS.—THE BISHOP'S PRIVATE CHARACTER ASSAILED.—
HIS TRIAL AND CONDEMNATION.

IN these reminiscences hitherto my memory has been occupied
with the rise and growth, in the United States, of Tractarianism, or what is more popularly known as the Oxford Movement. We had, in truth, a little Oxford on this side of the
Atlantic. It was located in a little suburban appendix to New
York City, known as Chelsea. Its name was the General Theological Seminary of the Protestant Episcopal Church.

The Oxford Movement in the United States came in due
course of time and very naturally to a convulsive conflict, a close
grapple of controversial contention and angry feeling which agi-
tated Anglicanism throughout the whole country. The immediate occasion of this was the examination and ordination of
Arthur Carey, an account of which has already been given in
the third and fourth chapters of these reminiscences.

A very salient statement of the causes which led to this
struggle and of circumstances which aggravated the excitement
was thus given, at the time, in the columns of the *Quarterly
Christian Spectator* for October, 1843 :

"Such an occurrence as the ordination of Mr. Carey with the
protest of two eminent clergymen against him, on the ground
of his being in effect a Roman Catholic, became the town's
talk; and filled the newspapers, not only in the City of New
York but everywhere else. Nor did the news from Europe just
about those days help to divert the public attention from these
matters. The astounding progress of O'Connell's movement for
giving to Popery its natural ascendency in Ireland; the ad-

mired secession of one-half of the Established Church in Scotland; the universal agitation in England about Tractarianism, together with the University censure of Dr. Pusey himself at Oxford, gave to an ecclesiastico-religious question of this kind a new and surprising power of interesting the whole people."

It was impossible that so fierce a conflict could go on long without a break-up of Tractarianism, such as it was, for in point of numbers Tractarians were by far the weaker party. It is also impossible to describe this break-up without giving some account of the trial and condemnation of Dr. Benjamin T. Onderdonk, President of the Seminary and Bishop of New York. To this we devote the present chapter.

DR. BENJAMIN T. ONDERDONK.

The ordination of Carey made Bishop Onderdonk the central point of a violent storm. The bishop could not properly be called a Tractarian, he was rather a High-churchman; but believing the Anglican Church to have been established on a compromise in matters of doctrine, he was willing to give that compromise its largest latitude. This made him a great protector of Tractarians, whether clergymen or seminarians looking forward to ordination. He was no great favorite at our seminary, but all the Tractarian students in the institution recognized him as a protector.

His ordination of Carey now made him a target. Every evangelical zealot, whether bishop, priest, or layman, entered upon a war the success of which seemed to depend necessarily upon the downfall of the bishop. As for him, his Dutch blood was fully aroused, and until his character was undermined he stood the shock of battle like a veritable Van Tromp. The war against him was not carried on merely in social circles and in the columns of the press, and in multitudinous pamphlets arraigning his action in the ordination of Carey; it broke out openly and vigorously in the first convention of his diocese that met after the ordination. This was in the latter part of September, of the same year, at St. Paul's Chapel in New York City. It was the largest gathering of delegates in convention since the formation of Western New York into a separate diocese in 1838.

On September 28, 1843, Judge Oakley, chief-justice of the Superior Court, opened fire upon the bishop in full convocation by the introduction of two resolutions in themselves not at all unreasonable, but in view of all the circumstances quite out of season if the end which he proposed to himself was the restoration of peace.

The first resolution was that the delegates from New York to the next general convention should be instructed to procure such an authoritative interpretation of the rubrics as should settle the question whether clergymen have the same right as laymen to object to a candidate in response to the call of the bishop at the ordination ceremony.

The second resolution looked forward to the procuring of a canon providing that upon the application of two presbyters objecting to the fitness of a candidate, a trial shall be had with notice of time and place, so that the two objectors may be present, and that the answers to all questions put to the candidate shall be placed on record.

These propositions seem innocent enough. We must consider, however, the time and circumstances which called them forth, all the heated discussions to which Tractarianism had given rise both in England and America, the suspicions so rife in regard to the orthodoxy of the General Seminary, the examination of Carey so widely published with all its particulars, and above all, the startling protests of Drs. Smith and Anthon at his ordination so summarily and indignantly disposed of by the bishop. It then becomes evident that the introduction of these resolutions into the New York convention was simply

the casting of an additional firebrand into the Anglican communion.

The attack was foreseen by Bishop Onderdonk. His opening
address and the whole result of the convention show how well
prepared he was to meet it.

The principal speaker in behalf of the resolutions was John
Duer, Esq, a lay delegate from Dr. Anthon's parish of St.

JUDGE JOHN DUER.

Mark's, a zealous Low-churchman, and one of the most distinguished jurists of the country.
He was surrounded and sup-
ported by many prominent laymen, some of them lawyers like
himself. His manner in speaking is thus described by a friend
in an article published in the
New York American of October
2, 1843:

"We have rarely seen an
instance where the sense of the
holy place in which he ·stood
and of the sacred nature of the
topics he was discussing seemed more thoroughly to pervade
the mind of the speaker, and
to impart to him the mastery
over the impulses with which
he seemed struggling to a more
impassioned style and burning
thoughts."

It is difficult to pass without some notice the utterances of
so strong a man on an occasion so memorable. A pamphlet
published at the time by Harper & Brothers, and preserved in
the State Library, enables us to refresh our dim recollections of
Judge Duer's argument. We only give a few passages, select-
ing such as are most likely to interest our readers. In the
course of his speech, after having waived all personal application of any of his remarks to the chair (Bishop Onderdonk),

and making the supposition that a bishop might arise whose own mind should be deeply infected with the very errors against which, as a church, Episcopalians had protested, he said :

" I have already spoken of testimonials and preparatory examinations. The only apparent security is the required sub-scription of the candidates to our Articles of Religion, but what security is that subscription against those who believe in the innocence of mental reservation ? What security against those who have l een taught to interpret the Articles in a sense that robs them wholly of their Protestant char-acter, and renders them easy to be reconciled with the most obnoxious doctrines and practices of Rome ? Under such a bishop there would be no difficulty in finding candidates of the necessary pliability of conscience. Rome herself, acting upon the system that in other countries she is known to have pursued, would supply them. She would send her own emissaries into your church, and not only permit but command them to become its ministers. Far from considering their subscription to your articles as a crime, she would en-courage and reward it as an act of pious obedience : the end to be obtained would sanctify the means. In the present state of the church, viewing the actual progress of certain doctrines, and the multitude and zeal of those who have embraced them —remembering the caution with which these doctrines were first promulgated and the lengths to which their authors have now boldly advanced, it cannot be said with truth that the dangers of which I have spoken are so remote and improbable that it would be useless to adopt measures of precaution. A Romanist bishop in a Protestant church is no longer an improbable event."

A little later the speaker refers to Tractarianism, and to the New York *Churchman* in particular, as follows :

" The doctrines of the Tractarian writers of Oxford have, in certain quarters, been openly embraced—have been propa-gated in the diocese with unusual diligence and zeal, and in a journal which claims to be the legitimate organ of the church, have not only been avowed in their full extent, but have been defended and maintained with signal ability, skill, and learning."

He adds : " They have become a favorite study of the youth

in our seminary, the future candidates for orders, and by many of the younger clergy who have issued from the seminary they have been passionately embraced, and are now zealously propagated."

The distinguished orator took occasion to champion the rights of the laity, to which, in his view, Tractarianism was especially hostile. "If you would lead the laity," he said, addressing the chairman, "the laity must know where you are going. If you would govern their conduct, you must gain their confidence by convincing their reason. If you claim from them an implicit faith, the claim is sure to be rejected, and those who, properly instructed, would have been glad to follow, will be prompt to abandon you." Then, bringing his argument to bear specifically upon the resolutions, he concludes: "In one sense the spiritual powers of the bishop to ordain cannot be limited; he may ordain whom he pleases, but his power to ordain those who are to be received as ministers of the church is necessarily subject to such regulations as the church may impose. To deny this is to subvert the whole constitution of the church—is to demolish the edifice, in order to build the prerogative of the bishop upon its ruins. It is to make each bishop the pope of his diocese."

A remarkable feature of this memorable convention is the careful courtesy with which the chief combatants treated each other. It could scarcely be otherwise, for they were all gentlemen and bred to understand the laws of courtesy. Their expressions of mutual esteem, however, were simply formal. Like pugilists before a combat, they shook hands, well knowing the fearful encounter which was to follow.

The bishop opened the synod with great dignity and solemnity, not affecting to conceal his consciousness that a storm was brewing and that he was prepared to meet it. His words, however, were kind and offered no provocation to attack unless a manly defence of himself and of the presbyters who had acted with him at Carey's examination is to be considered as such.

"Wicked attempts," he said, "are making without to rend us asunder by jealousies, and to provoke the disunion of our happy communion. To meet this, be we all as one man—cling-

ing to Christ, his cross, and his church, let us resolve that we
will be one in order, in affection, and in all the graces of the
Christian faith."

In like manner Judge Duer, before closing his argument,
professed his desire for peace and proffered as terms of peace
the acceptance of the hostile resolutions for which he con-
tended. Addressing himself to the clergy and laity who had
already shown their opposition to the resolutions on the day
previous, by seeking to have them laid upon the table, he said:

"Will you reject our overtures of peace? Instead of receiving, will you dash from our hands the olive branch we tender?
We entreat you to remember that if by your votes these resolutions shall be rejected, it is upon you alone that the responsibility will rest; you and you alone will be answerable to your
church and to your God for the consequences that may follow."

These professions of a desire for peace sound well, but were
necessarily unavailing. The famous words so well uttered at
the beginning of our American Revolution may readily be
applied to the mutual declarations of amity so formally made
at this New York convention.

"Gentlemen may cry 'Peace! peace!' but there is no peace.
The war is actually begun." A bugle-note of war was sounded
when the seminary at Chelsea was first assailed and Carey's
ordination objected to. Some miserable details excepted, all
that followed was inevitable.

This Diocesan Convention of 1843 was the culminating point
in Bishop Onderdonk's career. He stood at that time the foremost bishop in an ecclesiastical body comprising many distinguished priests and prelates. He was in that body the most powerful, courageous, and reliable champion of the High-church party.
Although much that occurred at that time has faded from my
memory, the long years have obliterated little of the picture
then imprinted of that fearless, ready-witted, and sagacious
man. He confronted his enemies in the convention at every
point. They retired from it at its close beaten and baffled.
And this was not caused by any insufficiency on their part, for
they included in their number some of the foremost men of
the day, flowers of the clergy and pillars of the bar. The tri-

umph of the evangelical cause came later and was achieved by
less respectable means.

To explain my meaning it will be necessary to give the
reader a sketch of the initiation and progress of a movement
against Bishop Onderdonk's private character. This was carried
on at first in secret, but afterwards was brought out in the
form of public charges preferred by his enemies and resulting
in his trial and condemnation by an ecclesiastical tribunal.

The first combined efforts of the Evangelical party of Anglicans against Tractarianism in America had been directed against
the General Seminary in Chelsea, and only included Bishop Onderdonk as president and professor of that seminary, and the
best-known defender of the rights of Tractarians to hold their
principles in the Anglican fold, to exercise their ministry in that
fold, and to use the advantages of the seminary.

The institution was governed by an ample Board of Trustees, to which all the bishops belonged *ex officio*. The attack began during a meeting of the board assembled at the seminary
for the June examinations of 1843. Drs. Smith and Anthon
proposed to the trustees that the examining committee should
direct their attention especially to points involving Tractarianism,
in order to draw out any bias of the students in this direction.
The trustees declined to do this on the ground that the business of the committee was not to examine, but to attend upon the examination as conducted by the professors and to report the result. Drs. Smith and Anthon were, however, added
to the examining committee, and it was suggested to them that
a request to the professors to examine any particular student
or students with special distinctness on any particular topics,
would undoubtedly accomplish their object. This course, we
are informed, was taken; but nothing appears to have been
elicited by this means either to prove or disprove the suspicions
which had been excited. Drs. Smith and Anthon were not satisfied with the manner in which the resolutions moved by them
had been disposed of. Still less were they satisfied the next
day, when a third resolution, requesting that the sermons which
the members of the senior class had handed to the professor
for inspection might be brought to the committee, shared the

fate of its predecessors and was laid to sleep with them. (See *Quarterly Christian Spectator* for October, 1843.)

This direct attempt of the Evangelical or Low-church party to purge the seminary of tendencies Romeward was soon discontinued for a less direct but more effectual method of warfare. Bishop Onderdonk, as we have said, stood foremost as the protector of Tractarians. He was fearless and powerful. To prostrate him would leave the cause he favored demoralized and without a head. There were existing circumstances which seemed to pave a way to effect his ruin, by assailing his character.

The first suspicions that the bishop's private life was open to attack on its moral side began to circulate about the time that I first came to the seminary, namely, in 1842. This appears by the testimony of the Rev. Paul Trapier, the record of which may be found in a pamphlet published by that gentleman in 1845, directly after the Onderdonk trial. I do not think the students of the seminary knew anything of such rumors until they were made public by the action of his prosecutors.

Mr. Trapier tells us that these rumors were well known among the presbyters of South Carolina gathered in convention in February, 1844. Mr. Trapier himself, who was prominent among these, was also a trustee of the General Seminary at Chelsea, New York, and an active Evangelical. He is well known to all who remember these sad transactions as the most active, untiring, and unrelenting of the bishop's adversaries. Three other presbyters are mentioned in his pamphlet as associated with him in bringing to light the evidence of misconduct relied upon by the presenting and prosecuting bishops. Two of these presbyters I knew personally. One of them, Mason Gallagher, was with me at the seminary during my first year, and was at that time a candidate for orders from Western New York. Gallagher is still living, a minister of the Reformed Episcopalians. Another was the Rev. James C. Richmond, already mentioned in our sixth chapter and bearing, as there stated, the sobriquet of "Crazy Richmond."

The convention of the South Carolina Diocese, in February,

1844, joined in the attempt already referred to by passing a re-solution to inquire into the state of the General Seminary. Rumors were already rife, as we have said, against the personal character of the Bishop of New York, but were not publicly in-troduced into the proceedings of this convention. They had their influence, however, upon these proceedings, as Mr. Tra-pier informs us, and helped to secure a majority in favor of the action there taken. He says:

"My conviction is that though the alarm was more extensive on the subject of Tractarianism, yet there could not have been the majority requisite for any action of the convention had not others of its members been uneasy about the moral influence of the Right Reverend Professor. As it was, the two sets of per-sons combining, such majority was secured."

Mr. Trapier himself tells us that he was not very apprehen-sive of Tractarianism infecting the seminary, and that he was not much disposed on its account to carry out—any further than duty might demand—the resolution of his convention. The ru-mors concerning the moral misconduct of Bishop Onderdonk were, in his view, more serious as they were rapidly spreading among the laity. He arrived at the General Seminary for the meeting of the Board in June, 1844, with a determination rather to make a special investigation into these private rumors. He returned home, so he tells us, without any success. No one could be found to stand to his assertions, none could allow the seal of confidence to be broken, and yet many were whispering.

At the next General Convention of the Church, which met at Philadelphia, and which Trapier attended, he was seemingly no nearer to his purpose than before. But one day, during the sessions of this convention, he was in the yard of St. Andrew's Church when he was informed by Mr. Gallagher that affidavits could be procured. The two resolved to consult Mr. Memmin-ger, a lay deputy from South Carolina, and found that he was already better posted than themselves, and intended to bring the matter out in open convention on the question of receiving the report of the trustees of the seminary. Instead of this, however, after consultation they concluded to put the matter into the hands of the bishops only, and they drew up and signed a memorial which was handed to Bishop Meade. A few days after Bishop Chase returned the paper to Mr. Trapier, the bishops having decided to present the matter in another shape. The reason assigned was that the conduct of Onderdonk as professor could not be inquired into without involving his character as bishop. Nothing was publicly done at the meeting of this General Convention. It is not probable that anything effective upon Tractarianism or the General Seminary or Bishop Onderdonk could have been done in General Convention, so long as his private character remained unassailed. The evangelicals, therefore, took the matter into their own hands. A trial of Bishop Onderdonk for immorality was determined upon. Bishops Meade, Otey, and Elliott undertook to present the case, and the time was fixed upon. The bishops would not consent to hunt up evidence, as one of them expressly declared to the Rev. Mr. Trapier. Trapier tells us that he thought this rather hard on the signers of the memorial; for he as one of them "had certainly had no expectation of being called upon to do more than put the bishops as a body into the way of getting at information by calling before them the clergymen whose names were therein mentioned," and that he "did not at all relish being transformed, though in a righteous cause, from the sufficiently odious position of an informer into the one yet more so of a prosecutor." The bishops, however, persisted, and Trapier and Memminger consented to the parts assigned them, Memminger acting a lawyer's part in receiving testimony and preparing affidavits, which work was done in New York.

The foregoing facts, gathered from Mr. Trapier's pamphlet, seem to me important to these reminiscences, as they show how the immediate field of war was transferred from the seminary to more secret action elsewhere, and finally to the scenes of the memorable trial of the New York bishop.

The proceedings of the actual trial of Bishop Onderdonk were all published, and therefore well known to me as well as to the entire public. Of this preliminary work, however, of hunting up evidence and of urging witnesses to come forward I should have known nothing at the time had I not accidentally become acquainted with the Rev. James C. Richmond, whom I have already mentioned as very forward in the movement. He talked freely of the part which he had taken in it.

There is good evidence to show that the bishop could have conciliated this adversary if he had thought it prudent and proper to do so. This we learn from Mr. Richmond himself, in his "Reply" to the pamphlet entitled "Richmond in Ruins."

The bishop is quoted as having made the statement that Mr. Richmond had called on him, and expressed a warm desire to return from Rhode Island to the diocese of New York, that he might be the bishop's friend and stand by him in his troubles. This is partially confirmed by Richmond himself. He states that he said to Dr. Onderdonk: "Bishop, are you aware that it is in my power to render you more service than any presbyter?" The bishop, he tells us, instead of saying, "What do you mean, sir?" blushed and was silent.

One who would have been very insignificant as an active ally was thus permanently made into a most dangerous foe. It was a repetition of the old story of Paris and the Tendon Achilles.

The court of bishops for the trial of Onderdonk convened December 10, 1844, in the Sunday-school building of St. John's Chapel, New York City.

Philander Chase, Bishop of Illinois, being senior bishop, was in the chair. Bishop Ives of North Carolina, Bishop Hopkins of Vermont, and twenty other bishops were present. Rev. Bird Wilson, D D., of the seminary, was unanimously elected secretary, which office, be it remembered to his great credit, he declined. Bishop Whittingham acted instead as clerk and secretary. Presentment was made by Bishop Meade of Virginia, Bishop Otey of Tennessee, and Bishop Elliott of Georgia.

The prosecuting bishops, as also Bishop Onderdonk, were represented by counsel, eminent lawyers of New York City. The presenting bishops were represented by Hiram Ketchum and Girardus Clarke. Bishop Onderdonk chose for his counsel David B. Ogden and David Graham.

The charge against Bishop Onderdonk, made by the presenting bishops, was that of immorality and impurity, nine separate instances being specified. No attempt to commit any criminal act was either proved or alleged. The offences proved consisted rather of maudlin familiarities indulged in by a half-conscious man overheated with wine, and generally before witnesses the fact of whose presence precludes all suspicion of criminal intent or any definite purpose. It was impossible for the counsel of the accused bishop, or for his friends, to make any complete and satisfactory defence of his conduct. It was easier, however, to palliate these offences and to show that his guilt was far less than his enemies would make it out to be. None of the instances alleged against him had occurred within two years and a half of the trial.

Under all the circumstances of the case it seems strange that such strong measures should have been taken, and that any number of Episcopalian bishops should have been willing to bring such scandalous matter to so public an exhibition. Ladies of high respectability and perfectly innocent were brought out in open court to testify, to their own confusion, and all that they said was paraded in the public newspapers. The proceedings of this extraordinary court, including the testimony of witnesses and the full arguments of the counsel, were published, by authority of the bishops themselves, in a pamphlet of three hundred and thirty-three pages, and a copyright secured. One young lady implicated in these disagreeable matters absolutely refused to appear and testify. Her name, however, and the nature of the insults offered to her all went freely before the public and appeared on the record of the proceedings.

The court remained in session during twenty four days, *i.e.*, from the tenth of December to the third of January inclusive. On that day the judgment of the court was publicly announced, in which the respondent was declared guilty of six of the charges specified by a majority of the court, consisting of eleven bishops. The verdict of guilty having thus been reached, it became necessary for the bishops to decide what the sentence of the court should be, namely, whether the punishment should be deposition, or suspension, or only admonition. The votes of the bishops on this question were given by ballot, each bishop signing his own name and sometimes also assigning on the ballot his reasons for the mode of sentence which he approved. There were several ballotings without arriving at any conclusion. Several of the bishops then changed their votes. Some of them gave as their reason for this, the necessity of securing a majority for some form of censure. Some of Bishop Onderdonk's friends, who voted at first for a simple admonition, ended by agreeing to a sentence of suspension to ward off a more serious censure.

Suspension was the sentence finally arrived at and declared by the court.

This sentence was never removed. A Standing Committee was empowered to represent temporarily the ecclesiastical authority of the diocese. Finally, in November, 1852, Dr. Wainwright was consecrated to take charge of the see, with the title of provisional bishop. This qualified title he continued to bear until the death of Bishop Onderdonk, which took place April 30, 1861.

The influence of this downfall of Bishop Onderdonk upon Tractarianism in the United States, both at the Seminary and elsewhere, will be presented and pictured to the reader in chapters still to come.

CHAPTER X.

BREAK-UP AT THE SEMINARY.—PROFESSORS TAKE ALARM.— JESU-
ITS IN DISGUISE.—WAITSON AND DONNELLY DISMISSED.—
McVICKAR WITHDRAWS.— WALWORTH, McMASTER, AND WAD-
HAMS CROSS OVER TO ROME.

THE trial and degradation of Bishop Onderdonk, of New
York, was a substantial triumph for the Evangelical party
in the Protestant Episcopal Church. It effected in the United
States in many respects what the condemnation of Ward had
brought about in England, although accomplished by different means. In England it was a square, open fight. It was
made evident that the Mother Church there would not tolerate
any further advance of Tractarianism, and this spirit prevailed
even amongst High-churchmen of every variety of color and
degree. The High-churchmen in the United States, however,
had not taken so much alarm. Hitherto they had resisted all
the efforts of evangelicals to meddle with the situation of things
at the General Seminary. They had with great unanimity sustained the ordination of Arthur Carey, believing that all the
leanings of Carey towards Roman Catholic doctrine and
customs were at least things to be tolerated in the same way
that the leaning of evangelicals towards the doctrines and
fashions of dissenters found tolerance.

So confident were the High-church bishops of maintaining
the toleration that they desired for their own views and for a
very large latitude in those views, that they ventured sometimes to indulge in a very humorous vein when dealing with
the alarm felt by the opposite party. This sportive mood displayed itself sometimes even in their General Conventions. In
the convention held at Philadelphia in October, 1844, Bishop
Chase presiding, it was proposed to send certain questions to the
faculty of the Chelsea General Seminary in order to ascertain if

Tractarianism was not propagated at that institution with the connivance and even with the open aid of some of its professors. From the autobiography of Professor Turner (page 192) we learn that forty questions were prepared and forwarded from the House of Bishops.

Some of these questions ran as follows :

"Are the Oxford tracts adopted as text-books in the seminary ? Are they publicly or privately recommended to the students? Is *Tract 90* used as a text-book, or (so) recommended ?"

"Are the works of the Rev. Dr. Pusey, Messrs. Newman, Keble, Palmer, Ward, and Massingberd, or any of them, used as text-books, or publicly or privately recommended in the seminary ?"

"Are the superstitious practices of the Romish Church, such as the use or worship of the crucifix, of images of saints, and the invocation of the Blessed Virgin, and other saints, adopted, or publicly or privately recommended in the seminary ?"

The questions just given emanated unquestionably from spirits of the Low-church type. They are ridiculous when the character of any of the professors of the seminary in my day is taken into account. How much fun was to be found among the right reverend bishops convened at Philadelphia may be gathered from the following questions, which were put in to serve as foils to the mischievous thrusts of the Low-church prelates :

"Is Calvinism, comprehending what are known as the ' five points,' so taught or recommended? Is any one of the five points so taught or recommended ?"

"Are the works of Toplady, of Thomas Scott, and John Newton, and Blunt on the Articles, or any of them, used as text-books, or publicly or privately recommended to the students of the seminary ?"

There is not so much fun in some of the other questions which intimate at the seminary the teaching of rationalism. These seem to be aimed chiefly at Professor Turner. There cannot be the slightest justice in them. Out of deep respect for the memory of that learned scholar and truly good man, I deeply regret them. They belong, however, to the history of the time, they are quoted by himself in his autobiography; no call of delicacy requires me to leave them out.

"Is the German system of rationalism—that is, of rejecting everything mysterious in the doctrines and institutions of the

PROFESSOR SAMUEL H. TURNER.

Gospel, and making human reason the sole umpire in theology, adopted or so recommended in the seminary? Are German or other authors who support that system adopted as text books, or so recommended as guides of theological opinion?"

Had the opponents of Bishop Onderdonk left his private character unassailed, they would have gained nothing in their war against the seminary or the stout old Bishop of New York, who was a champion too doughty for any honorable weapons which they could bring to bear upon him.

As it was, however, they conceived that they had scored for the time being a substantial triumph in accomplishing his degradation and suspension. Many churchmen who had stood by the bishop in defence of Carey were not prepared to justify, nor willing to appear before the public as justifying, all that was proved against the bishop on his trial. They felt humiliated in his humiliation. They felt demoralized and in a way discouraged. They became afraid to identify themselves with him in anything, even in what they believed to be right.

All this made a great difference with matters at the seminary. Our principal defender, the Bishop of New York, had now become defenceless. Those professors there who were either friendly to us or naturally indisposed to listen to anything which could disturb the seminary now became timid. They would gladly have shielded Tractarian students, but dared not. Professor Ogilby, on the other hand, though professedly a High-churchman and intolerant towards dissenters, was in his way a good deal of an Orangeman and always ready for a fight against anything that was really Catholic. He was now ready to take the lead in purifying the seminary of all Romanism. He soon succeeded in making things lively at Chelsea. He took it into his head that there was an organized party both in the seminary and outside, including clergy, whose object was to Romanize the Episcopalian Church.

One day near the close of December, 1844, Professor Ogilby sent for one of the students named Wattson, of the middle class, and accused him and several other students of being engaged in this conspiracy. The manner in which this suspicion arose I never knew until lately. The particulars have been furnished me by Wattson's own son, the Rev. Lewis Wattson, of Kingston, N. Y., with permission to use his communication freely. His father, Joseph N. Wattson, one day jokingly said to Prescott, who subsequently became a member of the English Society of St. John the Evangelist, known in the Anglican Church as the Cowley Fathers: "Don't you know, Prescott, that there is a number of Jesuit students in disguise here at the General, and that when they have made all the converts they can, they are going openly to Rome themselves?" Prescott took the joke in dead earnest and reported it to the dean. Upon this Watt-son was called up before the dean. In due course of time he, and another student named Donnelly, of the same class, namely, that of 1846, were publicly tried upon charges founded upon this misconception. They were acquitted for want of sufficient proofs, but for all that they were quietly dismissed.

The other students implicated by name in this supposed plot were Taylor, Platt, McVickar, and myself. Of these Platt was a graduate belonging to the diocese of Western New York and already in orders. Of Taylor I have no special recollections, though he belonged to my class. I find his name included in a list of alleged conspirators named by McVickar in a letter written at the time to my friend Wadhams, afterwards Bishop of Ogdensburg. This letter I have given nearly in full in my Reminiscences of Wadhams. I myself was at the time not in the seminary, although nominally a student still. I was resid-ing during the latter part of that autumn, and during the winter and spring of 1845, with Wadhams in the Adirondacks. He was in deacon's orders, having charge, under Bishop Onderdonk, of Essex County. His principal stations were Ticonderoga, Port Henry, and Wadhams' Mills. I did not belong to the jurisdic-tion of Bishop Onderdonk, but had received from him a license to act as lay-reader. This empowered me to conduct the morn-ing and evening service as provided in the Book of Common Prayer in the absence of my friend, as also to read a discourse from any book of sermons published by some clergyman of the church in good standing.

I do not remember to have read in public anything except from the "Plain Sermons," which were discourses of simple practical piety intended to be free from points in controversy and unobjectionable to any Anglican congregation.

McVickar, mentioned as one of the partners in this complot, was a son of the Rev. Dr. McVickar of Columbia College, one of the most learned of the clergy of the New York diocese and one of those examiners of Arthur Carey who had decided in his favor.

Henry McVickar had his trial before the faculty on the seventh of January. A special charge was made against him of recommending Romish books, and of believing in the papal supremacy. In the letter above mentioned McVickar states that the information came through P——. This may be the same student upon whom Wattson played his perilous joke.

It does not appear that anything was made out against McVickar at his trial, except that the latitude of opinion which he had used was detrimental to the interests of the seminary. His judges furthermore alleged that not McVickar, but they themselves were the best judges of what was thus detrimental. This claim McVickar allowed, and said that if they would point out how they thought he had injured it, he would avoid it for the future. Afterwards he thought he had allowed too much, for they restricted him so closely that he felt himself thoroughly hampered by his own promises and preferred to leave the institution. He retired to rooms in Columbia College, where he prosecuted in private his preparation for orders. He did not count, however, upon receiving orders at all. In a letter to Wadhams, dated Maundy-Thursday, 1845, he says: "I am extremely doubtful whether I can obtain orders without exciting new commotions and troubles; and if I think so when the time comes I shall not apply for them."

Whitcher (Benjamin F.), belonging like myself to the Western diocese of New York, was also involved in these troubles, although, being a graduate and in deacon's orders, he was no longer responsible to the faculty of the seminary. On a visit to New York at the time, he informed his friends there that he had been summoned to appear before his bishop. All those supposed to be in this popish conspiracy were reported to their several bishops. It is certain that Bishop De Lancey gave little heed to the charges made against myself. He never spoke to me or wrote to me on the subject. In fact I never knew that I had been denounced to him except through McVickar's letters. For this confidence in me I feel grateful to him; I have never ceased to cherish his memory as a loved and honored friend of my youth.

Dr. William Everett, now rector of the Catholic Church

of the Nativity in New York City, name loved and revered by all, then residing not far from the seminary and within easy reach of the students, a post-graduate of the last class, was as much a papist as any of us, but I cannot find that he was at all involved in this alleged conspiracy. I suppose the reason to be that, like Arthur Carey, he was considered too valuable a man to lose whatever his religious tendencies might be.

One thing connected with this complot is and, I fear, ever will be a profound mystery. Who could the concealed Jesuits be? Among all the faces at the seminary, still familiar to my memory, I cannot recall one that fills the picture. Shall we look for them among the faculty? It could not be Bishop Onderdonk, the president. He was bold, open, and outspoken in maintaining the right of Tractarians to toleration in the Anglican fold. But boldness and frankness are not the supposed characteristics of jesuitism, and he would never have been selected by that terrible society to act in such a capacity. Dr. Turner could never be suspected of acting in such a *rôle*. He was a most devoted student of the Bible, and so familiar with it that he seemed to know it all by heart; besides this, although not averse to quoting from the early Fathers in the interpretation of Scripture, he leaned more to modern Anglican commentators, and especially to such German authors as he considered to be reliable critics in matters of biblical text. Moreover, as dean of the faculty, he took not a little part in this very scare of which we are speaking. Professor Ogilby was a most violent anti-popery man and hated Romanism more even than he scorned Dissent. Professor Haight could not have been one of them. If so, he died in the same disguise. Good Dr. Moore must be acquitted of any such suspicion. Although learned in the Hebrew and gifted as a poet, he was as simple and hearty a man as Santa Claus himself. Moreover, while teaching us Hebrew from the Hebrew Bible, he made it an invariable rule, as being a layman, never to interpret the passages he translated. By this rule he cast away, as a concealed Jesuit never would, his best opportunity to poison our minds with popery. The only two left about the institution who had any easy access to the students were Professor Bird Wilson, who taught theology, and a good old man who presided over the coal-bins and furnaces. One gave out doctrines more or less new to us, and the other furnished fuel and fire. If these were Jesuits, they concealed themselves most effectually. No suspicion ever fell upon either of them.

Among the students themselves I can recall only two that can possibly lie open to suspicion. One had been a Catholic. He did not always give the same reasons for having joined the Episcopalian Church. Sometimes he alleged that it was because when he was a Catholic he was not allowed to read his Bible. This made him very interesting to a society of pious ladies who maintained him at the seminary. He told McMaster once that it was because he couldn't stand the fasting imposed upon him in the Catholic Church. This roused McMaster's indignation, who confronted him with the first reason given, insisting upon it that he should stand upon one story or the other, and say whether he had come over to Protestantism for the love of his Bible or for the sake of his belly.

The other student had been brought up in the Greek Church, and consequently early imbued with all that is held to be odious in Catholic doctrine except the supremacy of the Roman See. This one redeeming trait stripped him of horns and hoofs and made him welcome to Protestantism. Even thus, however, he might be a concealed Jesuit, but I am not aware that any such suspicion fell upon him.

The sensitive dread of Jesuitism which prevailed about this time, and had succeeded at last in placing a time-honored institution under public surveillance, was not confined to Chelsea, nor to the Episcopalian Church. It showed itself amongst other Protestant sects. A professor of an Eastern college one day enlarged before his class on a subtle policy attributed by him to the Church of Rome of locating Jesuit spies wherever an opportunity was afforded of doing mischief. "They locate themselves," said he, "in every city, every town, every community, every social circle, with an eye upon every family. I should not be surprised to learn that there is a concealed Jesuit, perhaps in this very institution, perhaps in this class-room at this very moment." The impression made upon the students was not a very solemn one.

That Break-up of Tractarianism at the Seminary to which I confine myself in these reminiscences as closely as possible, for the sake of preserving the necessary *unities*, was not precisely coincident with the general tide of conversions, either in England or in America, which carried so many Tractarians into the Catholic Church.

In a series of lectures delivered at London by John Henry Newman, in 1849 or 1850, he compares the great break-up of Tractarianism to an incident related in the *Arabian Nights*, when Sindbad, the sailor, and his companions found themselves stranded on what they took to be an island, but was in reality the back of a sleeping whale. The merry crew amused themselves in dancing, and shouting, and a variety of other antics on the back of the unconscious creature, and with perfect safety. When, however, they proceeded to build a fire upon his back the great fish woke up to a sense of pain and, becoming conscious that mischief was going on, he shook himself suddenly free from these disturbers of his peace. In England the Tractarian coals grew too hot for toleration when William George Ward, at Oxford, published his *Ideal of a Christian Church.* Ward's speedy condemnation followed, and all the Tractarians who really meant anything by their Catholic antics were either obliged to take refuge in the real Catholic Church, or else reconcile themselves to those quiet slumbers so congenial to their Anglican mother.

The break-up of Tractarianism in the United States was simultaneous with that in England. In the Mother Country and in the Mother Church the coals on the whale's back lay hottest at Oxford, and there the first nervous shock of the sleepy old creature made itself felt. The Seminary at Chelsea was the Oxford of American Anglicanism, and there occurred also the first throes of that convulsion which forced so many enthusiastic young Tractarians either to climb back into the Protestant ship and stay quiet, or else take to the water and swim for their lives.

One student had already left and united with the ancient church before the whale began to flop. This was Edward W.

Putnam, of the class succeeding mine. His conversion occurred in 1844. It took place so quietly that many of us did not know of it when he left us. Even now I do not know any details to show the special reasons and circumstances which led to his conversion. About three years afterwards he took priest's orders in the Catholic Church. I think he must have been ordained for the diocese of Albany, for I find his name in the parish records of St. Mary's, Albany, officiating under Bishop McCloskey during the first year of his pontificate in that diocese, after that prelate's transfer from New York. He was a good, zealous, and fervent priest, and his memory still remains in benediction among the few Catholics of Albany who are old enough to look back to his time. The latter part of his life was spent in Maine. He was a fruit of the Tractarian movement, but he does not belong to that great break-up of which I am now speaking.

The first conversion consequent upon the great scare at Chelsea in January, 1845, was my own. I was not at the seminary when the scare took place, although my name was involved in the supposed conspiracy. Its influence upon my life, however, was almost instantaneous. The reader must here recall the pretty little by-play of founding a monastery which Wadhams and I, in connection with McVickar, were carrying on among the Adirondacks in Essex County. This air-drawn convent of the future went down at once into the ocean when the scared fish shook his sides and dived. McVickar crawled back at once into safe quarters. Our beautiful *Fata Morgana* disappeared like a dream. Prior Wadhams, although suddenly unfrocked, still held his mission in Essex County and could take time to feel his way out. But I was completely afloat. Crawl back like McVickar and others, I would not. Go forward in pure dreamland, without a single peg to hang a hope on, I could not. Neither could I go home to my father's house at Saratoga, and to the village circle which surrounded it. There the atmosphere was more stifling even than the sham pretences to Catholicity so rife in Episcopalian Protestantism. Besides this, my Tractarian course had been so contrary to the wishes of my parents and other old friends near the homestead, that it seemed to me a call of honor to become independent, and by earning my own living acquire a right to follow my own conscience. The monastic bond between myself and Wadhams being broken, there was nothing to keep me any longer by Wadhams' side. Our vocations lay along different lines, and I must strike out a separate path for myself. I therefore made arrangements to work at a lath-mill in Essex County until I could see my way distinctly to join the Catholic Church, and enter its priesthood. Before I could carry out this plan, McMaster arrived at Ticonderoga on his way to Canada, and my friend and I went down there to meet him. On learning my determination to become a Catholic, and my preliminary purpose of becoming a miller's boy, McMaster said :

" Don't do that. I can tell you where to go. I've stumbled on a priest in New York City that is just the man to receive you into the church. It is Father Gabriel Rumpler. He is the superior of a convent of Redemptorist priests in Third Street, New York. He is a most remarkable man, full of learning, wisdom, experience, and a truly holy man. And besides that, it is an order of religious missionaries. You were always wild after missionary work. You can't do better than join them."

The account he gave of Father Rumpler and of the Redemptorists put an end at once to my project of going into the lath business. It opened a practical door by which to enter the Catholic Church. It promised me a wise Ananias to take me by the hand and direct my course among the new faces which were soon to gather around me, and in the new life which lay before me. My determination to become a Catholic was fixed and resolute. To unite with the Catholic Church all I needed was an introduction to it. The opportunity was now offered and I embraced it immediately.

Wadhams and McMaster accompanied me from Ticonderoga village to the steamboat dock by the old fort to see me off. I urged the former to take the same step without delay.

" Don't hurry me, Walworth," said he ; " I am in a position of responsibility and confidence, and when I leave, if leave I must, it shall be done handsomely. You have no charge. You have only to let your bishop know what you are about doing, and then do it."

"Go ahead, dear old boy," said McMaster. "I'm ashamed to have you get the start of me, but I'll follow you soon. I've been fooling about with these Puseyite playthings too long. Look for me in Third Street when I get back from Montreal."

There we parted. I took the steamer for Whitehall. Mc-Master took the same boat on its return and made his visit to Canada, and Wadhams went back, lonely and desolate, to his room at the village inn at Ticonderoga Falls.

A couple of days later found me knocking at the convent door in Third Street. I found in Father Rumpler the very man I needed. The Redemptorist convent and church were wooden structures at that time and very shabby. Everything was new and poor. I liked it all the better for its destitution.

During my stay in New York I stopped with my sister, Mrs. Jenkins, who resided with her husband and children in Eleventh Street, near the corner of Fifth Avenue; but I visited the convent in Third Street every day. Father Rumpler examined me very particularly, to see how near my religious convictions were in accord with Catholic faith and how far my intelligence of Catholic doctrine extended. My answers were satisfactory, and he said: "I see no reason to delay your reception into the church. Is there anything in Catholic doctrine which you find difficult to believe?" I answered: "No, father. I do not understand Indulgences, but whatever that doctrine really is, I am willing to take it on trust without the least doubt that whatever the church believes and teaches is true." He smiled and said:

"Well, that has the true ring of faith. You can take your time to study up that question, and now about your baptism."

I told him what I knew about my baptism when an infant by a Presbyterian minister; and the subsequent ceremony of trine immersion in the waters of New York Bay administered by my old friend, the Rev. Caleb Clapp. He said that the first baptism was probably done right and so valid, but if not, the second was superabundantly sufficient, and could not be made surer.

On Friday, May 16, 1845, I made my profession of Faith,

in the Church of the Holy Redeemer, in the presence of three or four witnesses only, and thus terminated at the same moment my connection with the Chelsea Seminary and with the Protestant Episcopal Church. On the following Sunday I made my first Communion at the same altar. Shortly after I was confirmed at St. Joseph's Church, on Sixth Avenue, by Archbishop Hughes.

In the meantime McMaster had arrived at New York. He took up his quarters with the Redemptorists, and was there received into the church. Both of us had come also to the determination to embrace the religious life in the Redemptorist Order. About the middle of June I went to visit my parents at Saratoga, where I remained two or three weeks. I then returned to New York, and on the 2d of August I set sail, in company with McMaster and Isaac Hecker, for the novitiate at St. Trond, in Belgium.

It is scarcely necessary for me to give any further details concerning the conversion of McMaster and that of Wadhams, since that would be only to repeat what has already been published at some length in my " Reminiscences " of the latter. I may be excused in like manner for observing the same reticence in regard to my friend, Henry McVickar. He never became a Catholic. He died, not long after his leaving the seminary, still an Episcopalian and in deacon's orders. Another of the same family, Lawrence McVickar, more happy than Henry, found his way into the Catholic Church at Chicago, or Milwaukee, during the sixties. He was a nephew of Dr. John McVickar, of Columbia College, and therefore a first cousin of my old friend and fellow-seminarian. He also died young.

In my next chapter I propose to continue my account of the great break-up of Tractarianism in the United States, introducing especially what I remember or have ascertained of other old companions at the seminary whose names have been introduced to the reader in these Reminiscences.

CHAPTER XI.

THE BREAK-UP (CONTINUED).—DIVERGING PATHS.—DONELLY.
WATTSON.—EVERETT.—PLATT.—WHITCHER.—AMERICAN
OBEDIENCE TO LAW.—BLIND OBEDIENCE.—THE CHELSEA
BREAK-UP ECHOED IN MARYLAND.—HEWIT, BAKER, AND
LYMAN.

ONE of the principal students at the seminary suspected of Romish tendencies, and even of being engaged in a complot against the interests of the seminary and the peace of Protestant Episcopalianism, was James B. Donelly, of the class of 1846. As I have already stated, on his trial before the faculty he was acquitted for want of definite proof, but was for all that obliged to leave the seminary. Dr. Seabury befriended him, and found employment for him in the office of the New York *Churchman.* Perhaps, also, Donelly served, as Carey had done before him, as assistant to Seabury in the little old Church of the Annunciation, since known as St. Ambrose's, on the corner of Thompson and Prince Streets.

I had some correspondence with Donelly while he was thus engaged in New York and I was residing with my friend Wadhams in Essex County, before my entry into the Church Catholic. I sent him an article which I wished to have published in the *Churchman.* The spirit of the article was altogether too hot for even Dr. Seabury to handle, as he informed me through Donelly, who urged me to come down to New York and have a talk with the doctor about it.

Later, after my profession of faith, Donelly made a visit to the Redemptorist Convent upon my invitation, made acquaintance with Father Rumpler, and looked at the church and convent buildings with great interest. He seemed much depressed and under great restraint, more so when talking with me than when in conversation with Father Rumpler. Whether

the extreme poverty which prevailed everywhere was repugnant to him or not I cannot say, but he returned no more and
I never saw him again.

It is certain that shortly after this last interview of ours
Donelly had it in his mind to enter the Catholic fold, but
needed encouragement to carry it out. One day when passing
by the Catholic Cathedral on Mulberry Street, in company with
Wattson, his classmate and co-conspirator, he proposed to the
latter to make a call on Archbishop Hughes. Wattson hesitat-
ed for awhile, but finally declined the offer, and the golden
opportunity of grace passed away from both for ever. This
incident I have from Wattson's own son, now rector of St.
John's Church, Kingston. In an interview with this latter gentleman he communicated to me many incidents derived from
his father concerning these early days, with full freedom to
publish all he communicated. His father said to him once:
"Had I accepted Donelly's invitation at that time and visited
Archbishop Hughes, there is little probability that either you
or I would now be Episcopalians."

Some things communicated to me by Wattson (the younger)
he put down on paper, for I feared to trust my memory too
far. Among these I find the following:

"Donelly, on leaving the seminary, was ordained by Bishop
Onderdonk and was assistant to Dr. Seabury. Pressure becoming too great, he was forced to leave New York and so far
ostracised that he took some out-of-the-way parish in the South
and shortly after died."

From all that I can hear of James B. Donelly, he died a
broken-spirited man. He was naturally too much of a man to
thrive while trampling upon his conscience.

Joseph N. Wattson, after being dismissed from the seminary, sought his Diocesan, Bishop Lee of Delaware, who
calmly told him, "Young man, my advice to you is: go to
Rome, for that is where you belong." He was finally ordained to the priesthood in the diocese of Maryland, by Bishop
Whittingham. He afterwards went to Mississippi, but at the
breaking out of the Civil War returned to Maryland and remained there until a few years before his death, which occurred

in Kingston, New York, in 1887. By a singular coincidence Bishop Lee ordained to the diaconate in June, 1885, the Rev. Lewis T. Wattson, now rector of St. John's Episcopal Church, Kingston, New York—and he was presented by his father, Joseph N. Wattson, whom Bishop Lee years before had advised to go to Rome.

William Everett, known familiarly amongst us by the name of Doctor, was as far advanced as any of us in Tractarianism, but was of a prudent and quiet disposition, besides being highly esteemed for his scholarship, wisdom, and high moral qualities. I cannot remember that he encountered any difficulties in the way of his graduation or receiving of orders. He did not enter the true church until 1850 or 1851. I met him for the first time after my own conversion, and after my return from Europe, while engaged in giving a mission at Saint Peter's Church, Barclay Street, where he visited me.

It was a great joy to meet my old companion again and greet him as a Catholic. He is still on duty as rector of Nativity Church in New York, over which he has presided for many long years.

My cousin, Charles Henry Platt, one of those included with me in the charge of conspiracy against Anglican Protestantism and the interests of the seminary, was, at the time, a graduate and already in orders at Rochester. He was then as near to Rome as man can come without actually crossing the gulf. When Bishop De Lancey, of the Western diocese, received my letter asking him to take my name off from his list of candidates, he said to Platt, "What will your cousin do? Will he go over to Rome?" Platt answered that of course I would. His manner was so indignant and the words he added were so full of contemptuous bitterness for the thraldom in which he felt himself enwrapped, that the bishop felt it necessary to employ every means to hold him to his chains. Several of Platt's letters to Wadhams may be found in my "Reminiscences" of that good bishop. They show how near he then came to his salvation.

A short time before my departure for Europe and the Redemptorist novitiate, I wrote to my cousin urging him to come to New York and see me off. He replied that he could not come. That to do so would involve a decision to leave the Anglican communion, and that he could not break his mother's heart by taking such a step. I have lost his letter and remember in general only its substance. The state of his conscience is clearly shown in the first words of the letter, which I remember very distinctly. It began thus:

"DEAR COUSIN: I thank my God that your feet are at last planted upon the 'Rock of Peter.'"

Poor man! He lived to marry and have a family. He served as chaplain in the army of the Union. He never became a Catholic. At the time of his death, in 1869, he was rector of Christ Church, Binghamton, N. Y.

The influence of my cousin's example was very unfortunate upon his classmate, co-conspirator, and most familiar friend, Benjamin W. Whitcher. I had sent to him a similar invitation to come and see me before I left for Belgium. At first he was inclined to do so and endeavored, though in vain, to engage Platt to accompany him. Of this he informed me in his reply, saying also that he could not venture to come alone. When denounced, as we have seen, for his Romanizing tendencies, he was summoned to his bishop for examination, and there was a delay about his ordination. A letter of Platt's dated April 6, 1846, which is given in the "Reminiscences" of Wadhams, tells us something of this affair. We read as follows:

"Whitcher is in priest's orders. He had a hard time winter before the last. They passed him to the priesthood last fall; but he was plump with them, and kept nothing back."

Whitcher must be classed amongst that large number of Christian workers, apparently very zealous at first, who are covered by our Lord's rebuke when he says, "No man putting his hand to the plough, and looking back, is fit for the kingdom of God." His first backward step was when he took orders in the Episcopalian communion. The second was when he took a Presbyterian wife. Still later on, becoming a widower, he took a second wife, and became surrounded by a family of children. Ten years of his life passed away in this false position when, much shorn of his former strength and demoralized by loss of self-respect, he found his way into the Catholic Church. I will give in detail that part of his conversion with which I had something to do.

In 1855, if I remember rightly, I was engaged in giving a mission at St. Patrick's, Utica. Whitcher, at that time, had charge of an Episcopalian church near by at Whitesboro.' One day a card was brought up to my room bearing the name of my old friend upon it. I soon had him by the hand. I anticipated a warm discussion, for I have never found any Protestants more fierce in controversial fencing than old Tractarians who have backed away from their earlier convictions. I was therefore resolved, if possible, to get in the first thrust. After he had taken his seat and we had got past the first natural greetings, I said:

"Well, Whitcher, don't let us dodge the one great matter we are both thinking of. Why are you not a Catholic long before this?" Without showing the least signs of fight, Whitcher dropped his head and answered:

"Sure enough, that is the great question, and I don't know how to answer it."

"Ten long years of your life have passed away," I continued, "and still here you are, looking one way and rowing the other. How can you do it? How can your conscience bear it?"

"Conscience!" he repeated mournfully; "don't talk of conscience. I don't know that I have any conscience left."

His case was a plain one. I urged him to do his duty manfully and without further delay. To this he agreed. "Only give me two or three weeks," said he, "to settle up a few affairs, and I promise you that I will then go to Father McFarland and put myself in his hands." This promise he carried out faithfully. Father McFarland, then in charge of St. John's Church, Utica, is now well remembered as the third bishop of Hartford, Conn. Whitcher has published a full history of his conversion, giving his religious life as Presbyterian and Episcopalian. In this will be found some account of his connection with the break-up at the seminary, and his examination before his bishop. It is called "The Story of a Convert, as told to his former parishioners after he became a Catholic."

I do not think that the incidents thus far given or any others that I may give tend to show anything like a spirit of disobedience to superiors in young Tractarians or any others in America who followed the Oxford movement. Whatever those educated under European influences may think of us, the virtue of obedience and respect for rightful authority comes as easily and naturally to true Americans as to any other people. The great crisis which most threatens the prosperity of our country at the present time is one which shows foreign lawlessness reaching to anarchy combined against American law and order. So long as Americans remain American, nihilism and anarchy imported from abroad will have to bow before the majesty of law. And let me add, the more that Americans study the Catholic Church and its religion, from her own doctrines, from her own decrees and her own authors, the more they will find that true obedience and true liberty are twin sisters. At the bottom of this whole matter lies the primary question: In what does the true virtue of obedience consist?

I have the following incident from Father Isaac Hecker, late superior-general of the Paulists. It came to him from the lips of Cardinal Barnabo, who was so long Prefect of the Propaganda in the days of Pius IX. Once, when presenting and recommending to that Pontiff an appeal from an American religious against his superior, the Holy Father said:

"What shall we think of these Americans? Do they understand obedience?"

The cardinal replied:

"I do not think they know much about *blind* obedience. I do think, however, that they understand what true obedience is, and that they practise it as well as any other people."

Another incident goes more thoroughly into the question. I have it from Bishop Lynch of Charleston, one of the most learned and gifted prelates that our American hierarchy ever knew. He was a student at Rome in the time of Pope Gregory XVI.

A young American had been admitted into the English College there, and held a room in the building during the rectorship of Dr. Wiseman, afterwards cardinal. He had nearly completed his course of studies when a young Englishman of a distinguished family applied for admission into the same college. It was full. The rector endeavored to make place for him by persuading our American student to give up his room and pursue his studies privately, promising him that he should graduate like the rest and receive his diploma.

The student replied that he did not value his position in the institution simply for the privilege of a diploma, but was particularly anxious to have the benefit of the whole course of studies. For this reason he declined to withdraw. He persisted in this determination notwithstanding all that the rector could urge, and although a day or two was given him to consider. Dr. Wiseman then took a short and decisive way to enforce his will. On returning to his room one morning the student found his door locked and all his furniture moved out into the corridor. No remedy was left him but to appeal to higher authority. He did appeal to the Cardinal Prefect of the Propaganda. The cardinal was surprised and displeased. He considered that the young man had been wronged. He promised to see him restored to his rights, and appointed a day when he should call again.

When presenting himself again on the day appointed he did not find the cardinal prefect so resolute. He was told that Dr. Wiseman was a very eminent man whose standing and influence at Rome were very high. It would be far more prudent and advisable to yield to his desires, instead of persisting in an opposition which would be almost sure to prove fruitless. The unfortunate appellant saw that he had little to hope from the present appeal.

" I will not trouble your eminence any further," he said, " in this matter, if you will promise to do me one favor, which will cost you very little. Will you obtain for me a private audience with the Holy Father himself?"

This promise was readily given. At the audience thus obtained the Holy Father listened with great attention, noting down carefully certain particulars. "I will make further inquiries into this affair," he said, " and that at once. Give me your present address, and leave all the rest to me."

It was not long before some of the Papal *sbirri* appeared at the English College and moved all our student's furniture back into his room. This, of course, settled the whole matter so far as that case was concerned. Another point, however, was settled in the mind of the English rector.

"So long as I am head of this college," said he, "no Americans shall get into it again. *They won't obey anything but law.*"

I have always taken great pleasure in this anecdote because I consider it to be highly complimentary to the American character. I am free to confess that blind obedience finds little favor in this country. St. Francis of Sales, when conversing one day with certain young sisters of the Order of the Visitation on the virtue of obedience, was asked what they should do in case one of their superiors should give some order that would be contrary to the laws of God or of the Church? Francis replied that in that case they should not obey her, any more than if the superior were to say, "Sister, go into the garden and gather some flowers, and throw yourself out of the window that you may get there the sooner," when the sister should gently and respectfully answer: "Mother, if you please, I will go down the stairs."

I have already said that the progress of the Oxford movement in the United States, although generally adverse to a blind obedience, was not characterized by a spirit of disobedience, though this was frequently charged against some of them by their bishops and other superiors. We have seen something of this overstraining of authority in the experience of Henry McVickar at the Chelsea Seminary, which led to his withdrawal from that institution. Some of the bishops in their dioceses carried on things with a much higher hand. I will here refer to a few instances with which I am most familiar, or which are most accessible to me. Let us begin with the diocese of Maryland.

William Rollinson Whittingham was one of the foremost figures of the Episcopalian communion at the period of which I am treating. He graduated at the Chelsea Seminary in 1825, and officiated as professor of ecclesiastical history from

1836 to 1840, when, being made bishop, he moved to Baltimore and assumed charge of his diocese. I am glad to introduce Bishop Whittingham to the reader, not only because of the im-

REV. DWIGHT LYMAN.

portance of his diocese and of his own personal eminence, but because, so far as he dared to be so, he was a Tractarian. Arthur Carey had been one of his pupils at the seminary. After Carey's ordination Whittingham endeavored to secure him for his diocese, but without success. Several young men, however, not unlike Carey, soon gathered around the new bishop and looked up to him as a guide and protector. Three of these, afterwards converts to Rome, are especially memorable. Dwight Lyman became an inmate of his family. When Lyman went to Hagerstown to pursue his studies at St. James's College, Nathaniel Augustus Hewit took his place with the bishop's family, in Courtlandt Street. Directly opposite, on the same street, resided Francis Baker. The bishop's demands upon the obedience of these three rare young churchmen were remarkable, and remarkable was their docility. Father Hewit says in his Memoir of Baker:

"In Bishop Whittingham's own eyes, he was himself the equivalent of the whole Catholic episcopate. Consequently, what he and his colleagues and predecessors in the Anglican Church had decreed had full Catholic authority, and was just as final and authoritative as if the whole world had taken part in it. Hence the assertion of a despotic, exclusive authority of the Anglican Church, concentrated in his person, over every one who acknowledged his jurisdiction. He would not permit us to attend any Catholic services, or read any Catholic books, as an ordinary thing." Hewit was anxious to read Möhler's *Symbolism* and Ward's *Ideal of a Christian Church*, but did not do so on account of the bishop's prohibition. He even gave up using certain Anglican books of devotion to please him. Hewit says: "Baker was equally obedient with myself at that time; although afterward, when he was governed more by common sense and a just sentiment of his own rights, he read whatever he thought proper."

The compliance, however, which Bishop Whittingham and other Episcopalian bishops of his type required from their neophytes was not so much an obedience to law, for Episcopalianism in the United States has very little ecclesiastical law to back it up. The bishop stands in the midst of his clergy only as *primus inter pares*. He is superior in dignity rather than in power. He has not much authority of a kind that can be enforced. He can neither appoint a rector to a parish nor remove one from his charge. He has no cathedral properly so called ; that is to say, a seat, or see, in any mother church around which the other churches of the diocese cluster as dependencies. The actual state of things is illustrated by the fact that in New York for many years the bishop occupied the position of assistant minister in Trinity Church. So at Baltimore Bishop Whittingham, who for a long time was rector of no church there, had no authority in any of the churches. He could not, for instance, officiate or preach at St. Paul's Church, in Charles Street, without permission of Dr. Wyatt, who was the rector.

There is, however, another kind of authority not founded on any canonical law, which Episcopalian bishops often claim, and is carried even farther in that denomination than in the Catholic Church. It is simply that authority exerted over the opinions, actions, and general life of others founded upon a deference to some superiority in age, office, dignity, or experience ; or upon a combination of these qualities in a class of prominent men. It often has no other sound reason to enforce it than the *argumentum ad verecundiam.* In the Anglican Church this sort of authority was liberally and often successfully employed to keep young Tractarians from going to Rome, or otherwise following their consciences in the ruling of their lives. In my "Reminiscences" of Bishop Wadhams I have shown what warning letters were addressed to him, urging him to yield the dictates of a conscience already thoroughly enlightened to sagacious guides and politic trimmers who had no authority to appeal to but grave beards and pompous phrases.

This solemn *cantiloquia* went very far in the diocese of Maryland. Bishop Whittingham himself was so far committed to Catholic innovation in matters of outward form that it was hard to drive his young colts with a safe and steady rein. He was himself the first to wear long cassocks, reaching nearly to his heels. He could not quarrel with his neophytes if they wore theirs a little longer. This caused them sometimes to be mistaken for Catholic clergymen. One day on Saratoga Street Baker, when passing by two boys who were playing together on the sidewalk, was saluted very reverentially by one of them. Baker felt pleased, but was soon taken down by the other boy, who cried out:

" Hello! What are you taking your hat off to? That ain't no priest. What's the matter with you?"

Baker felt at the time as if he had been caught in a sort of fraud, but often told it afterwards as a good joke.

The bishop at the same time favored also the use of crosses in the churches, the removal of pulpits towering above desks and communion tables underneath, and the substituting of something in their place more like altars. Hewit, Baker, and some others eagerly followed the bishop's lead, and would gladly have pushed their imitation of Roman observances much farther. This they could not very well do at St. Paul's, where they attended, for Dr. Wyatt was omnipotent there and clung to the more Protestant practices in which he had been brought up. There they contented themselves with kneeling with their faces towards the altar, though the rest of the congregation faced the other way. Providence soon opened a better way to play Catholic. They came to know a well-disposed rector of a rather small brick church in a poor district of Baltimore. He warmly sympathized with Hewit and Baker in their Catholic tendencies, and allowed them to remodel the interior of the church and to imitate Catholic ceremonies according to the full desires of their heart. This liberty they carried so far that the congregation became alarmed and remonstrated ; and as the bishop seemed indisposed to interfere, they began to forsake the services. The parish was threatened with ruin both spiritual and financial. At this juncture a power more effectual than that of the bishop interposed. This was the rector's wife. With her it was a matter of bread and butter, and she interposed her authority so effectually that all the innovations were brought to a stop. The obnoxious symbols on the window curtains were banished out of sight. The chancel was restored to its former simplicity, containing no longer anything bearing resemblance to an altar, but revealing as before the old marble-topped communion table which, like so many others, would have served as well for a washstand.

Hewit, Baker, and Dwight Lyman, whose names we have brought so prominently forward amongst the Tractarians of Maryland, must not be set down as characterized by a spirit of ritualism.   Outward forms have often real value as symbolizing essential doctrine, and therefore minds most earnestly seeking for doctrinal truth must needs often attach much importance to ceremonies.   The cross is typical of the atonement, the altar of a continued visible sacrifice, and rich and costly vestments, when attainable, are acknowledgments of the presence of God in the temple.   But these young men cannot be classed with

VERY REV. A. F. HEWIT, D.D., C.S.P.

those who place ceremony, dress, or any show above truth and true worship, or place quaint fashions or antique curiosities above sincere and heartfelt devotion.   It was an easy thing for them to yield up cassocks or Roman collars when their bishop de-sired it.

When the time came for Hewit's ordination to the diaconate he gave his assent to the Thirty-nine Articles in the sense of

"No. 90." Baker was passed for ordination to the priesthood by the bishop, despite his unqualified rejection of Articles 22 and 31, besides some others.

It was not long before Whittingham himself fell under suspicions of popery, and was obliged to defend himself against the open attacks of one of his own clergy, the Rev. Henry V. D. Johns, rector of Christ's Church. It was to avoid the charge of popery that he put an end to the very novelties which he himself had introduced. Paralyzed by this change of front on the part of their bishop, many of the clergy and students dropped quietly back into the old ways. Some who felt it hard to keep quiet left the diocese.

Hewit, Baker, and Lyman yielded much at first. It was not long before they found their consciences put to a far severer test. They were expected to abandon what they felt to be the only way to truth. This brought them speedily to a decisive "break-up," like that which took place at the Chelsea Seminary. Hewit was the first to take refuge in Rome. His conversion followed close upon that of John Henry Newman in England. He was received into the Catholic Church at Charleston, S. C., in 1846, at the close of Holy Week.

Baker, whose attachment to the Anglican Church reached farther back, lingered several years longer. He was received into the Catholic Church by his old friend and comrade, Father Hewit, April 9, 1853. The reception took place in the little chapel of the Orphan Asylum of the Sisters of Charity, in Baltimore. I was then residing at the Redemptorist Convent in Saratoga Street, and saw him in his visits there during the days of his preparation. My memory is still fresh with the keen interest I took in the conversion of a man already so distinguished. Baker was ordained to the priesthood September 21, 1856, in the Baltimore Cathedral. Present on that occasion and in priestly vestments was Dwight Lyman, his old friend and co-partner in so many vicissitudes of joy and grief and trials of conscience. A few days later Hewit, Lyman, and Baker celebrated together a solemn votive Mass of thanksgiving at St. Alphonsus' Church, for the same great grace.

CHAPTER XII.

IN the last chapter I have attempted, according to my feeble means, to show how the break-up of Tractarianism at the Chelsea General Seminary was echoed in the rest of the United States and particularly in the diocese of Maryland. There the bishop of the diocese was a High-churchman, inclined to favor Tractarianism, and was, intellectually speaking, the leading mind among that class of bishops. If his courage had been equal to his inclinations, he would have been beyond all question the "great gun" of his class. The Low-church party had also its "great gun," equally well loaded and more apt to go off. This was Charles Pettit McIlvaine, second Bishop of Ohio, who succeeded to his diocese in 1832.

The peculiarity of his evangelical views may be accounted for by the fact that he was educated at Princeton, and was a professor at a very similar institution, the University of the City of New York, at the time when he was selected for the bishopric of Ohio.

One of his earliest appointments after ordination was to St. Ann's Church, Brooklyn. The call to this church came in 1827. While there we find him taking part in the formation of an evangelical society or conference of clergymen belonging to New York City and vicinity, called the Protestant Episcopal Clerical Association. The object of this association was stated in its constitution to be the promotion of the personal piety and official usefulness of its members, by devotional exercises and by conversation on missionary and other religious subjects.

This enterprise was promptly squelched by Bishop Hobart as something likely to prove mischievous, something that might lead to "cant" and perhaps to a partisan influence. The word "cant" I quote from Bishop Hobart. One of its members being a professor at the General Seminary, it was thought that this influence might be extended to the students.

Some members of the association afterwards grew up to higher views. McIlvaine never did. In his whole life and doctrine I can find nothing characteristic of Episcopalianism except that he used the book of Common Prayer, and attached some importance to Apostolic Succession. Baptismal Regeneration he scouted, while he was in no respect behind Calvin in maintaining the doctrine of "total depravity," or behind Luther in his extravagant presentation of the great Protestant heresy of "justification by faith only."

While a student in the seminary I went one Sunday morning to hear him preach on this last doctrine, which was his favorite theme. I think it was at St. Mark's, on Eighth Street. It made the blood fairly creep through my veins to listen to him. This must have been in the early summer of 1843, when he was on a visit to New York, soliciting aid for his institutions at Gambier, Ohio. It falls within my purpose to give the reader some idea of these institutions. It will show the bishop such as he was in his own domain, at work in the seat of his power, with his principal materials for good or evil near at hand, surrounded by his clergy and neophytes. We shall then be better able to understand what a formidable adversary to Tractarianism was such a man, so fortified by his position in public life, so animated by intelligence and energy of character.

In a published appeal for financial aid, dated New York, June 27, 1843, he tells us that the principal buildings of the institutions at Gambier were the residences of the bishop and of the president of Kenyon College, and five professors' houses. The students of the college paid for their instruction, but the course at the seminary was free. A village had grown up at this location. The whole tract of land consisted of four thousand acres. Thriving farms were scattered about where only a few years before nothing could be seen but a primeval forest.

Much of this reminds us of the growth of Nashotah at about the same period, leaving out the longings of Breck and his companions for the ancient faith and for monastic seclusion.

Bishop McIlvaine had at that time in his diocese fifty-nine clergymen. Of these, twenty-seven were educated in part or entirely at Gambier. Others educated in part or entirely there had moved out of the diocese. We know by other testimony that some left because the bishop made it too hot for them. Only one student of the General Seminary had come to him since his accession to the episcopate.

Dr. McIlvaine was not the sort of man to govern his diocese with a velvet hand. The direct powers of the episcopate are very limited in the Protestant Episcopal Church, but it was not his way to economize such power as he had. His temperament was polemical. Although rightly ranked as an evangelical, his spirituality consisted more in a protest against "good works" as having any intrinsic value than in a tendency to sentimental piety. There was a great deal of the Presbyterian in him, but he would have made a poor Methodist. He opposed himself openly to camp meetings and to all such revivals as either originated or resulted in breaking up the quietude of Christian souls.

His views on the subject of revivals are given in full and at length in a "charge" to his clergy delivered at Chillicothe, September 5, 1834. It is a strange thing that a Revival of the true Presbyterian or old-fashioned Congregational type should have taken place in his own college at Gambier, some five years later, the results of which were truly remarkable. We give an account of this Revival as written by the hand of an eye-witness, Mr. William Richards, who "got religion" on that occasion. It is taken from a public lecture of Richards' delivered many years later.

"It commenced," said the lecturer, "without preparation or special efforts—no one knew how; but it went on until nearly every student was counted as a 'convert.' The last month or two of the college year, 1839, was given up mainly to this revival, as the saving of souls was considered of vastly more importance than mere learning, or any other earthly interest. I allude to this event and mention the fact that I was one of the subjects, simply for the purpose of setting before you what was, and perhaps still is, the evangelical notion of 'getting religion.' 'Seekers' were diligently impressed with the notion that they must expect, seek, and pray for a 'change of heart.' And when, after a sharp struggle, sometimes short and sometimes lasting days or weeks, one could at last get up in meeting and say with tears of joy that 'At such an hour and such a place [possibly behind a big log in the woods, or in the loft of the barn, or in the closet if he has one, or elsewhere], while agonizing and praying to the Lord, suddenly light came in upon his soul, and he was convicted and felt happy!'—then he was regarded and received as a convert. He had 'experienced religion'; he was no longer a mere worldling; he had come out from the world; the old Adam was put off; old things had passed away and all things had become new! While this excitement lasted there was a happy state of feeling. But it is not in the nature of man to keep up that excitement continuously. The tension must give way, and lassitude and coldness follow. Then came in many cases the surprising and painful discovery that the change of heart was not a radical change after all—that the old man Adam was not conquered and put off, and that it was still just as easy as of old to be wicked, to get angry, to lie or swear, or slander, or have bad thoughts, or be worldly minded."

I have given the above details simply to furnish a picture in a general way of the state of things in a Low-church diocese at the period of which I treat. I have given also the ordinary characteristics of an evangelical or Low-church bishop presiding in such a diocese. In this case, however, it must not be forgotten that the bishop happened to be, not merely a type of his class, but the leading evangelical bishop of that day, towering in intelligence, energy, and importance above every other Low-church bishop. The following sketch of the man has been given to me by one of his own clergy, now a Catholic layman, Henry L. Richards, of Winchester, Mass. I have seen the bishop and heard him preach. I have a very vivid recollection of that occasion. I remember very well, also, my own con-

ception of the characteristics of the man derived from others
and stored away in my memory. I cannot pretend, however,
to place him before my readers in such true colors as those
furnished me by this venerable convert, who was educated

HENRY L. RICHARDS.

under the bishop's own eye at Kenyon College and Seminary
and was even a favorite pupil. Mr. Richards is still, at the age
of eighty years, after a laborious life in business, in the full
vigor of his remarkable faculties, active in charities and literary
pursuits. This is what he says of Bishop McIlvaine:

"The bishop was in many respects a remarkable man. He had a good deal of religious fervor and enthusiasm, and a great horror of Popery. He was arbitrary, dignified, and not very accessible except to his particular friends and sympathizers. He was interesting and effective in his extemporary sermons and addresses, but his formal written discourses were rather stilted and heavy."

Amongst all evangelical enthusiasts, especially ladies, Bishop McIlvaine was a hero, a sort of apostolic divinity. I remember well the worshipful words of an excellent Presbyterian lady of New York City already introduced to my readers. Anything clerical was to her something angelic; even I, boy that I was, stood in her regard as something like Raphael's round-cheeked cherubs, with very little wings put on to atone for cheeks and eyes extraordinarily human. But Bishop McIlvaine, though most violently and bitterly evangelical, with his high talents and fine elocution, was something superhuman. "Isn't he perfectly wonderful?' she would say to me. "Isn't he lovely?" I could not enter into her enthusiasm at all, though I would willingly have done so, for she was very dear to me, and I was always glad to please her. I acknowledged that he was wonderful enough. I wondered at him myself, but I thought him altogether unlovely. I could very well have used the terms applied by the celebrated Rufus Choate in praise of a Massachusetts judge:

"We look upon him as a heathen looks upon his idol. We know that he is ugly, but we feel that he is great."

Of course, in such a diocese as Ohio, administered by such a man, Tractarianism could not have, comparatively speaking, any very great foothold.

The reader will remember, perhaps, the incident given in Chapter II., of the putting up in the seminary chapel at Chelsea of a cross surrounded with evergreens, preparatory to midnight services on Christmas eve. This the students were obliged to take down by order of Dr. Turner, dean of the faculty. We learn from the worthy doctor's own Autobiography, that this incident, apparently so trifling in itself, was brought before the public in consequence of a communication to Dr. Turner from the Bishop of Ohio, who had heard of this affair and wanted to be informed about it. Dr. Turner tells us that he gave Bishop McIlvaine an exact account of this matter in his reply, and consequently it became public. It was, moreover, made a subject of public ridicule, so the dean tells us, by a church paper. This looks like the work of Dr. Seabury of the *Churchman.* An English work entitled *Records of Councils* noticed the same affair with similar ridicule of the dean's action. Fun also was made of it during the General Convention of the Episcopal Church at Philadelphia in 1844.

There was very little of war against Tractarianism, either in private machination or popular excitement, where the shadow at least of Bishop McIlvaine's hand did not appear.

Henry L. Richards, already quoted, says of the atmosphere pervading the bishop's institutions: "There was no conflict in the seminary or college because he was careful to secure professors of his own stripe of churchmanship. There were several 'old-fashioned' High-churchmen (you know what that meant in those days) among the clergy, but they were careful not to render themselves obnoxious to episcopal authority. The bishop was always glad to get rid of High-churchmen and to fill their places with those who sympathized with him. He was apt to give the cold shoulder to all who taught the sacramental system, while those who preached the Calvinistic doctrine of justification by faith only received his warmest friendship."

But Tractarianism had found its way even into Ohio, at the time of which I am writing. And when the great break-up came at Oxford and at Chelsea Seminary, it brought trouble even to Ohio and to Bishop McIlvaine, while it introduced young men of high culture, great talent, and eminent virtue into the fold of the Catholic Church. Foremost amongst these were several members of the Richards family, of whom five now living are known to me. To the kindness of some of these I am indebted for a large part of what I have already written concerning Bishop McIlvaine and his diocese, and for what I have still to write.

I scarcely know where to begin the story, but perhaps it makes little difference. There was one parish in the diocese of

Ohio, almost if not absolutely the only one in the State, where High-church ideas prevailed. It was, at least, the principal and leading one of that sort. This was St. Paul's, at Columbus. Bishop McIlvaine thought it a matter of high importance to set a guard over this congregation, to keep it from spreading infection, and if possible to lead it into more evangelical paths.

In 1842 the bishop appointed to this charge a young man reared under his own eye, and moulded to his own thoughts and methods. This was the Rev. Henry L. Richards, already mentioned, a graduate of McIlvaine's Theological Seminary at Gambier, and an approved evangelical. He has said of his theological studies: "It was during the 'Oxford' controversy that we were under the bishop's instruction, and our principal text-books with him were a small volume on *Justification by Faith Only*, and a good-sized octavo on *Oxford Divinity*, which he wrote about that time to stem the tide Romeward, which he had the penetration to see was flowing rapidly in that direction."

It can easily be seen that such a young man was one after the bishop's own heart. So thoroughly had he become imbued with the bishop's sentiments that he had been allowed to preach his own sermons in the country around Gambier before he was ordained. But, alas!

> "The best laid schemes o' mice and men
>   Gang aft a gley."

Dr. McIlvaine was doomed to be disappointed in his man. St. Paul's congregation were not brought down to the evangelical tone, but their young pastor was ere long elevated to higher views of Christian faith, Christian worship, and the value of sacraments. The change came about after this wise.

In the congregation of this young church at Columbus one of the principal parishioners was Mr. Isaac N. Whiting, the well-known bookseller and publisher. Through the friendship and courtesy of this gentleman, Richards became better acquainted with the standard works and arguments of the High-church party. He was introduced to a new world of thought, in which

High-church authors spoke for themselves. In brief, the young pastor not only became a High-churchman, but passed rapidly through that unmeaning middle ground, and became a Tractarian. This change soon showed itself, not only in his sermons but was made manifest to the very eyes of the congregation in the altar and other fixtures of the church, and in various decorations. The marble-top communion table with desk above and behind it, and pulpit towering above both table and desk, were discarded and gave place to something more like a real altar, in appearance at least.

These things could not be kept long from the knowledge and attention of such a bishop as McIlvaine. He had not been contented up to this time in guiding the minds of his collegians and seminarians safely through the snares of pompous prelacy and wicked popery. His wrath against these things, already sufficiently kindled, had been blown into a white heat by the ordination of Arthur Carey. In a charge to the clergy and laity, at a convention of his diocese held in September, 1843, he had denounced Tractarianism and openly condemned the action of Bishop Onderdonk; and his prominence and rule in Ohio were so recognized that the convention had seconded this onslaught by resolutions passed unanimously.

In such circumstances the new altar at St. Paul's, Columbus, could not stand long. The young rector was ordered to take it down. He obeyed, albeit reluctantly and under protest. He sawed out the panels and made an honest table out of a mock altar that had no sacrifice. The bishop knew very well that, to all Episcopalian intents and purposes, a true washstand was as good as a mock altar, but his object was accomplished by this surrender of the young rector. There were several long and solid communion tables in the diocese besides that at Columbus, with embroidered covers or antependiums resembling piano-covers, but this one he was determined to make an example of as a Romish innovation. Thereby, moreover, he humbled a new and somewhat refractory young Tractarian. The young Tractarian is still living and full of life at the advanced age of eighty years, and able to laugh both at himself and the bishop.

The resolute bishop had still more thunder in reserve. The

priest of St. Paul's was a *caput notabile*. The other offenders could say to themselves, *Procul a Jove, procul a fulmine*, and besides this they could just as well be attended to a little later and one at a time. The bishop took occasion from the above incident to issue a *pronunciamento* against Roman altars in Protestant churches which attracted considerable attention and criticism at the time. Amongst his works may be found a pamphlet published in 1846, entitled "Reasons for Refusing to Consecrate a Church having an Altar."

In 1849 Henry Richard's health becoming poor he went to New Orleans. At this time he had become a Roman Catholic in belief. In the heat and enthusiasm of his new conviction he returned to his home in Columbus, Ohio, "expecting to carry with him to Rome a number of his devoted High church friends." In this he found himself grievously disappointed. This disappointment caused his own courage to fail. He still remained for two years lingering and afraid to make the great leap which is always necessary to bring one out of a false church into the true fold of Christ. These were the two most unhappy years of his whole life. In addition to the agony engendered in his own mind, his condition was embittered by the opposition of friends and the estrangement of his nearest kindred. It is not necessary to mention these painful things in detail. In the month of November, 1851, came a sickness unto death. He found himself in the bosom of his family prostrate and helpless, apparently just at the gate of eternity and yet outside the pale of that great church to which his faith clung and in which his heart lay. He called for a priest. His demand was refused. It so chanced that in this extremity he

"Found not a generous friend, nor pitying foe."

He had a brother, indeed, who sympathized with him, of whom more by and by. But that brother was at the time far away. Kind Providence here interfered, and in a manner as unexpected by our young Tractarian as by those who should have listened to the cries of his conscience and befriended him. The crisis passed away, leaving him still weak but rallying. The sympathizing brother came on the wings of the wind to his succor. This brother, named William, a younger man, but, like Henry, of advanced Catholic views and likewise a thorn in Bishop McIlvaine's side, proved for the time a successful peacemaker. He made arrangements to remove the patient to his own home in Newark, Ohio, where he nursed him until his recovery.

William had hoped to persuade Henry to delay the great step, and was prepared with many reasons for such delay. Precisely the contrary happened. The foolish *via media* grew meaningless before the strong light which Henry's mind and conscience were able to throw upon the questions which came into discussion between them.

On January 25, 1852, Henry L. Richards was received into the Catholic Church, and the great chasm was closed which had separated him for awhile from the home of his conscience. Fortunately this step did not separate him from his family, though it broke up his connection with the congregation of St. Paul's at Columbus, and with Anglicanism. He had acted as rector of this parish of St. Paul's from 1842 to 1852. When he sent in his formal resignation, Bishop McIlvaine was manly enough to say that he respected him a great deal more for his consistent action than those who had the same views and sentiments yet continued to remain where they were. A strong and conscientious man is always a thorn in the side of a superior who rules by an unwarranted authority. Under the circumstances, no wonder that the bishop felt relieved.

Being a married man with a family, the advent of Henry Richards into the Church closed up to him all avenues to a life in the priesthood. To a highly intellectual and theological mind like his this loss of a cherished career must have been a great sacrifice. But he made this sacrifice and others manfully, hopefully, and even cheerfully. He acknowledges that he had many trials to meet at first, but insists that he has always looked upon these as his greatest blessings. He entered promptly into business, beginning in New York City as clerk to Edward Frith, a Catholic gentleman, agent in America for Sanderson Brothers & Co., Sheffield steel manufacturers. His active, energetic life in this new vocation has brought to him in his old age comfort and prosperity, without diminishing his faith and piety, or his interest in all that concerns the welfare of Christ's Church or the happiness of his fellow-man. He is the centre of a family group of Catholics, including the wife of his youth and several children. One of these, his oldest son, is Henry Richards, edi-

WILLIAM RICHARDS.

tor of the *Sacred Heart Review*, published in East Cambridge, a prosperous Catholic paper. To this, as well as to other papers and magazines, he himself, at the advanced age of eighty years, is a frequent and valued contributor. His second son, William, is an enterprising and thriving dealer in iron and steel. His youngest son, the Rev. J. Havens Richards, S.J., is the well-known and honored President of Georgetown College, D. C.

Among other members of this numerous Catholic family of Richards is William, Henry's brother, of whom I have already had occasion to speak as once resident in Bishop McIlvaine's diocese, and concerning whom there remains more to be said.

William Richards, a little younger than Henry, and like him early placed under the dominant influence of Bishop McIlvaine, was also a student at Kenyon College, graduating with his brother in 1838. Although strongly religious, the natural bent of his mind was towards philosophy, and his pathway to religious truth from the errors of Protestantism lay along a weary course of philosophic wandering. After his graduation at college he remained at the institution for awhile making special studies in history, philosophy, and law, under the instruction of the Rev. Dr. William Sparrow, whom he terms a learned and competent teacher, although a radical Protestant. In 1842 we find him at the Yale Law School in New Haven, where he still kept up his readings in philosophy.

From these brief details I hasten forward in order to carry out my purpose of connecting him with the break-up of Tractarianism in the Ohio diocese. William Richards had carefully kept his eye, all this while, on the progress of his brother Henry towards Catholic truth, and sympathized with him strongly. It became his fate to take part also with that brother and others in troubling the peace of Bishop McIlvaine.

In the summer of 1844 he received and accepted an invitation from the faculty of Kenyon College to deliver an oration at the coming commencement. This took place in August.

It was a great occasion, and for any one interested in Ohio Churchmanship, with a desire in his heart to formulate his views, a most desirable audience. For William Richards, a pretty well fledged Tractarian, it was a bold thing to attempt formulating his at such a time and place. If Tractarians were present in his audience they were all well handicapped. He was or had been recently a law student at Yale, but Yale was not in the diocese of Ohio. His leaders in philosophy, Cousin, Lieber, Carlyle, and Brownson, were not represented there; still less Newman, Pusey, and Faber of Oxford, or Dr. Seabury of the New York *Church-man.* Kenyon College, however, was there, with a great part of its affiliation; and Charles Pettit McIlvaine, head of the college and seminary, and *facile princeps* of Low-churchism in the United States, was there in all his glory, and with far more than his full canonical power.

" He was the heart of all the scene."

It was in such a place, before such an audience, and in such a presence, that William Richards, a graduate of Kenyon, and still only a student, unlaureled in any profession, dared to intro-duce his philosophical and theological bomb-shell. His philo-sophical aberrations from current Evangelical tradition might, perhaps, easily have found pardon. Older men than he was are expected betimes to slip up in such matters. What Ameri-can cares for a few powder-crackers in a barrel? But why speak disrespectfully in such an atmosphere of private judgment? Why intimate that the sacred right of private judgment, so precious in the eyes of Protestant Evangelicals, and so strongly intimated in the Thirty-nine Articles, is inconsistent with the Twentieth Article, which puts forth in plain terms the following declaration to be subscribed by all the English clergy:

" The Church hath power to decree rites or ceremonies, and authority in controversies of Faith."

It is true that the Church of England has so little authority that she dares not attempt to hold a convocation to decide any question of faith or doctrine, and that she has never enjoyed this privilege since she was first begotten. She cannot even interfere authoritatively in matters of ceremony without permis-sion of the prime minister, or the sanction of the state Court of Arches. This is very true, but it only makes the presumption of young Richards all the more apparent. Private interpretation may be very uncivil although quite rightful. Such was, in fact, the general judgment that day at Kenyon College.

This oration embraced, moreover, one more telling point, one more novelty which startled not only the bishop but the whole audience. It was a sigh for unity, and that a unity from which was not excluded the ancient church, Catholic and Roman.

This remarkable oration was the topic of discussion at all the dinner-tables that day in Gambier, and the universal comment was: "That young man is on the road to Rome!"

At the end of his oration, as William Richards left the stage and walked down the aisle, he met a friend, a lawyer of Columbus, who was to deliver the next oration. He saluted Richards with the blunt question: "What did you mean by that oration?" The answer was: "I meant just what I said." "Well," said his friend, "I brought two orations with me—the best one on 'French Literature,' and the other on 'William Leggett,' and now I am going to give you a counterblast by giving the 'Leggett' document." This second oration proved to be as radical in politics as any Evangelical discourse could be in religion, but not quite so startling at Gambier that day as the utterances of Richards.

Among those present at these exercises was the Rev. George Denison. He was rector of the church at Newark, where Richards resided, and nephew of Bishop Philander Chase. It was a great annoyance to him at the dinner-tables that day to be obliged to admit to numerous questioners that the Tractarian orator was a parishioner of his.

William Richards fulfilled the prophecies so freely made concerning him on this commencement day which we have described. He became a Catholic. He lives amongst us now, one of the most honored names in the church's long list of educated convert laymen. A manuscript lecture of his delivered in 1887, before the Carroll Institute, for the benefit of the Brownson Monument Fund, has been generously put in my hands, and aided me much in the preparation of this chapter. I have only used such incidents and dates as lend themselves to my especial purpose.

Those who would study the great social problems of our day by the light given to a true Catholic made competent to speak from the bosom of a long experience, ripened by a careful and thoughtful philosophy, and by a truly spiritual faith which always recognizes duty both to God and man, should read the essay of this same William Richards of Washington, printed in the "Proceedings of the American Catholic Congress of 1889."

In the present chapter I have only picked a few seeds from the surface of a large field, confining myself to the locality of a single diocese and to a short period of three or four years memorable in my own life. Bishop McIlvaine, Gambier, with its theological seminary and Kenyon College, lie before us as plain as I know how to picture them. These are in contrast with Bishop Whittingham and scenes which surrounded him at the same period. Both these localities connect by wires with the Chelsea Seminary, which in many respects must be considered, at the period in question, as the centre of electric fire. It is a sort of drama that we have attempted to present, and trust that we have sufficiently preserved "the unities." The unity of action must be looked for in that momentary confusion which we Tractarian converts unwittingly united to produce. A sudden break-up came first. After that break-up there settled upon many grateful hearts in America a sweet and long-abiding peace.

FINIS.

www.ingramcontent.com/pod-product-compliance
Lightning Source LLC
Chambersburg PA
CBHW022357020726
47500CB00002B/320